SO-BRI-083

WORKING WITH LIBRARY BOARDS

A How-To-Do-It Manual for Librarians

GORDON S. WADE

HOW-TO-DO-IT MANUALS
FOR LIBRARIES
Number 17

Series Editor: Bill Katz

SCSU
H.C. BULEY LIBRARY

APR 1 3 1992

New Haven, CT 06515

NEAL-SCHUMAN PUBLISHERS, INC.
New York, London

WITHDRAWN

Published by Neal-Schuman Publishers, Inc.
100 Varick Street
New York, NY 10013

Copyright © 1991 by Gordon S. Wade

All rights reserved. Reproduction of this book, in whole or in
part, without written permission of the publisher is prohibited.

Printed and bound in the United States of America

Library of Congress Cataloging-in-Publication Data

Wade, Gordon S.
    Working with library boards : a how-to-do-it manual for librarians
  / Gordon S. Wade.
        p.   cm. — (How-to-do-it manuals for libraries ; no. 17)
    Includes bibliographical references and index.
    ISBN 1-55570-080-2
    1. Libraries—Trustees—Handbook, manuals, etc.   2. Library
administration—Handbook, manuals, etc.   I. Title.   II. Series.
    Z681.5.W33   1991
    021.8'2—dc20
                                                        91-37358
                                                          CIP

O
Z
681.5
.W33
1991

To the three most important people in my life:

Penny, Dave, and Helen

With Love

CONTENTS

PREFACE

Working With Library Boards: A How-To-Do-It Manual for Librarians focuses on the practical aspects of working with a board of trustees, committee, or group in control of a library—public, private, college, or school. Library boards can have a tremendous impact on the success or failure of a library, yet little information of a practical nature is available about the relationship between the library director and the library board. The formal education of a professional librarian rarely includes such material, and the real education of a librarian on this topic begins with his or her first director's job when the complexity of this relationship becomes apparent. The literature of librarianship offers little in this regard—the topic is all but ignored by the media. Most of the books written on the subject tend to be from the trustee's point of view rather than that of the library director.

Working With Library Boards seeks to remedy this deficiency. It is written in a straightforward manner so that librarians interested in improving their working relationship with their library board may do so easily. The emphasis is always on the practical as opposed to the theoretical. The tips and techniques offered in this book are ones I have used and found to be effective. The book attempts to put into writing what successful library directors practice when they work with their library boards or committees. I hope that these techniques will lead to more effective relationships between directors and boards which will, in turn, lead to better libraries.

Working With Library Boards should be viewed as a hands-on manual for librarians who must deal day-by-day with groups who legally control their destiny. Each library board is different but there is help here for the novice and experienced library director alike. A positive future for libraries depends, in large measure, on library directors and library boards working effectively with one another to present a united leadership to officials and the community.

I would like to thank a number of people who helped make this book a reality: Bill Katz, for asking me to write it; John Houlahan and the interlibrary loan staff at the Northwest Regional Library in Sioux City, Iowa; Gerry Rowland of the State Library of Iowa; the late Professor Fred Wezeman of the library schools at the University of Minnesota and later the University of Iowa, who always emphasized the practical realities of librarianship; the Board of Trustees and the Library Staff of the Carroll Public Library; Rebecca Drahovzal, of the University of Kentucky at Lexington, for her valuable research; my editors: Nancy Viggiano and Patricia Read of Neal-Schuman; and the 75 public library directors in the

United States and Canada who so graciously responded to my survey about library boards in the spring of 1991.

Gordon S. Wade

BOARD STRUCTURE

Library boards for public libraries are established according to the laws of the people. In order to function properly they need to have a framework within which to operate. State and local laws and ordinances provide the basic structure, and bylaws created by each library board allow it to function effectively.

STATE AND LOCAL ORDINANCES

State codes and local ordinances are the basis of the library board's power. This framework is usually incorporated into the board's bylaws, for it tells exactly what powers the board has and how they may be exercised. The local ordinances must not conflict with state law, and frequently the city code will merely repeat state laws as they concern the library within the city ordinances. Sometimes a city will amend its ordinances in an effort to gain some measure of control over an otherwise autonomous library board, and in doing so come into direct conflict with the state. This happened in Bloomfield, Iowa, in 1987 when the city adopted an ordinance requiring the library to comply with city personnel policies while state law limited city control of the public library to appointment of trustees and appropriations.[1] The library board appealed to the county attorney who asked the Iowa attorney general for a ruling. The ruling favored the Library because the state law was violated by the local ordinance.[2]

THE BYLAWS

The first article in a public library board's bylaws is usually the article of authorization, and it generally incorporates the exact wording of the state and local laws as they pertain to libraries. A typical authorization statement will include the following: the purpose of the article (to provide for the appointment or election of the board and to specify the board's powers and duties); definitions of the public library and the library trustees; the qualifications of trustees; the organization of the board, including terms of office, what to do when vacancies occur on the board, and compensation of trustees; powers and duties of the board; contractual agreements; use of the library by nonresidents; expenditures;

the annual report; and provisions for the handling of theft and damage of library property. Articles of authorization often have similarities from state to state, but they can also be quite different. In some states library boards have been abolished by the state, or laws have been passed allowing cities to eliminate library boards which have the authority and power to govern the local public library. In these instances, the library may become a pawn of the city and its management, and the library board, if it continues to exist at all, functions only in an advisory capacity.

Library boards operate less effectively without a set of up-to-date bylaws, and yet some library boards never get around to updating them.[3] The first priority for any new library director is to create bylaws where they do not already exist, or to revise the already existing bylaws. An annual review both in committee and by the full board is a sound practice and one the library director should insist upon. Resistance is often encountered from library boards who feel they can operate successfully without up-to-date bylaws. In these instances, the library director can only continue to point out the inadequacy of the bylaws and hope to encourage the board to reconsider its position.

OFFICERS

Other articles in the bylaws further define the way the board will operate. The article entitled "Officers" spells out which officers the board will use. For example: the bylaws of the Anytown Public Library's Board of Trustees state that "Officers of the board of library trustees shall be a president, a vice-president, a secretary, a treasurer, and a recording clerk." Naturally, library board officer requirements will differ from community to community—some may not need all the officers named above, others may wish additional officers. If the board does not control its own finances, a treasurer may not be needed. It is a good idea to record in the bylaws that the library director is the permanent secretary of the board. That way his or her presence at all meetings (except where otherwise specified by the bylaws) is guaranteed. Subsequent sections of this article will specify how these offices are to be filled, when elections will be held, what to do when vacancies occur, how long officers of the board will serve, and the duties of each office. For example, the following article is taken from the bylaws of the library board of the Anytown Public Library:

ARTICLE II. OFFICERS

Section 1: Officers of the Board of Library Trustees shall be a president, a vice president, a secretary, a treasurer, and a recording clerk.

Section 2: The office of secretary shall be permanently filled by the library director. The offices of president, vice-president, and recording clerk shall be elected at the annual meeting of the Board for a term of one-year. Vacancies in office shall be filled at the next regular meeting of the Board after the vacancy occurs.

Section 3: The office of treasurer shall be permanently filled by the Anytown city clerk, who shall not be required to attend meetings of the Library Board unless specifically asked to do so.

Section 4: The president shall preside at meetings of the Board of Library Trustees. The vice-president shall preside at meetings of the Board of Library Trustees when the president is absent. The recording clerk shall take the minutes of each meeting. The secretary shall transcribe the minutes of the meeting into the permanent minutes book and shall give notice in writing of all meetings of the Board. The treasurer shall write checks for all Library expenditures as authorized by the Board through its Ways and Means Committee. In addition to the foregoing duties, each officer shall perform the duties which, by custom and law and the rules of the Board, shall devolve upon such officers in accordance with their titles.

Section 5: Terms of all officers except secretary and treasurer shall be limited to two consecutive years.

Note that section 2 requires an annual election of officers and that section 5 limits all officers, except secretary and treasurer, to two consecutive one-year terms. The annual election of officers rule is a good one because it legalizes the changes and eliminates the possibility of one person serving as president year after year. Trustees vary in their abilities as well as their dedication to the library. It is better to make frequent changes in the officers than to retain the same officers for a long period of time. The position of president of the board is a powerful one and should be rotated among the members if at all possible; these bylaws force this change to occur on a regular basis. Other board offices are often tedious (like the recording clerk, for example), and it is good to pass these less desirable chores around as well.

MEETINGS OF THE BOARD

A third article in the bylaws of the library board legitimizes the meetings: their frequency, when they will occur, whether or not a certain meeting has a special designation (like the annual meeting, for example), the procedure involved in calling a special meeting, quorums, order of business, and parliamentary procedure. Again, using the Anytown Public Library's bylaws as an example:

ARTICLE III. MEETINGS

Section 1: The Board of Library Trustees shall meet quarterly each fiscal year. The first meeting of the fiscal year shall be designated the annual meeting and shall include the annual report, election of officers, and appointment of committees; the second meeting of the fiscal year shall be designated the budget meeting.

Section 2: Special meetings may be called by the president or upon written request of three trustees, for the transaction of business as stated in the call. Notice stating the time and place of any special meeting and the purpose for which called shall be given to each trustee at least two days in advance of the meeting.

Section 3: A quorum for transaction of business shall consist of a simple majority.

Section 4: Order of business shall be:

1. Call to order.
2. Reading and approval of minutes.
3. Approval of bills.
4. Correspondence.
5. Report of the library director.
6. Committee reports.
7. Unfinished business.
8. New business.
9. Adjournment.

Section 5. *Robert's Rules of Order,* latest revised edition, shall govern the parliamentary procedure of the Board.[4]

The frequency of board meetings varies from library to library, of course, but the number of regular meetings held each year must be specified in the board's bylaws. The board may wish to be more specific about the time of meeting, in which case the information must be included in this article. For example, the first sentence of section 1 could read as follows: "The Board of Library Trustees shall meet quarterly each fiscal year on the third Monday evening of the months of January, April, July, and October." Remember that the bylaws dictate the way the library board will operate, so they must be as general or specific as the board finds necessary.

Note that provision is made for calling a special meeting of the board. In this set of bylaws, the library director cannot call a special meeting without the permission of the board president. A single trustee cannot call a special meeting unless he or she can persuade the president or two other board members to agree with the need. This prevents the calling of unnecessary meetings and also prevents a single overzealous trustee from exceeding his or her authority.

It is important to know how many trustees constitute a quorum—a simple majority is the usual rule of thumb. Again, this must be stated in the bylaws. Equally important is the provision governing parliamentary procedure. This provision may never be needed, but if it *is* needed and the library does not cover it in its bylaws, problems may arise.

The order of business is also stated in this article of the bylaws. Once again, the order used here is just an example. A different order may be used in other libraries. One good reason to have it as a part of the bylaws is that it makes the meetings of the library board consistent—the trustees know what to expect at every meeting. Some boards have another item, a review of the agenda, in the order of business. This gives trustees the opportunity to add or delete items as necessary.

COMMITTEE STRUCTURE

Another article in the library board's bylaws concerns itself with the structure of committees. Section 1 may deal with the committee appointment process and list the standing committees of the board.

Section 2 deals with the power to appoint special committees and may simply state, in general terms:

> "The president shall have the power to appoint special committees, with the approval of the board, to undertake such projects as the board shall determine from time to time." This section allows the president to create special committees to deal with situations outside the defined responsiblities of the standing committees. An example of a special committee is one charged with setting up art shows periodically in the library's adult reading area. This committee could include a trustee as chairperson and three interested individuals from the community as members. It may function for years, until the board feels that the special situation has passed and the committee is no longer needed. It is important that the president's charge to appoint special committees is subject to full board approval. Sometimes a president will wish to appoint a special committee, but the board will vote it down. This provision needs to be a part of the written bylaws.

Section 3 is important because it sets the limits of each standing committee's responsibility. For example, the *Ways and Means Committee* at the Anytown Public Library shall have as its duty "to recommend policy to the Board of Library Trustees" in the following areas:

- The annual budget.
- Salaries and wages of library personnel, personnel classification, probationary periods, promotion, and retirement provisions.
- Holidays, vacation, and sick leave for director and staff.
- Payment of expenses for trustees and staff to attend conferences, workshops, and professional meetings.
- Payment of state and national association dues for board members, staff, and the library.

The areas of responsibility are specified, and also that the committee is to function only in an advisory capacity. It is not given the authority to make policy—only to recommend it. This fact is very important and must be stated in the board's bylaws.

THE LIBRARY DIRECTOR'S FUNCTION
One of the most important articles of a library board's bylaws is the one dealing with the library director. The library director needs

to know the limits of his or her authority as defined by the employer, the library board. The bylaws of some boards in this regard are very specific, but other boards grant the director broad authority and responsibility. An example of broad authority is the following from the Anytown Library:

ARTICLE V. LIBRARY DIRECTOR

Section 1: The library director shall be appointed by the board of library trustees.

Section 2: The library director shall be considered the executive officer of the board and shall have sole charge of the administration of the library under the direction and review of the board of library trustees.

Section 3: The library director shall be held responsible for the care of materials and equipment, for the employment and direction of the staff, for the efficiency of the library's service to the public and for the financial operation of the library within the limitations of the annual budget.

Section 4: The library director shall attend all board meetings, serving as secretary, except those at which the appointment, salary, or performance of the director is to be discussed or decided.

Section 5: The library director shall be required to recommend merit increases for the library staff. The board of library trustees shall set the salary and merit increases of the library director. All salaries shall be reviewed annually by the board of library trustees.

Section 1 gives the board the authority to hire the director. This authority is actually one of the charges to the board made by state law, and will also appear in the first article of the board's bylaws. Section 2 defines the library director's position and relationship to the library board. This section places the board and the director in their respective places in the library's chain of command. Section 3 grants the library director the authority needed to operate the library successfully. It is a broad charge which succinctly states the director's position, responsibility, and limitations. Section 4 is quite specific with regard to the director's function at board meetings. The final section of this article deals very directly with salaries and wages and, as shall be seen later in this book, contains the important provision that all salaries and wages will be reviewed annually.

"If the librarian and the board can establish early on a relationship in which they see themselves working together as a team, the support from the board will be there when it is needed, and the librarian will have the advocate for his or her support when it is needed."[5]. The concept of the library director and the library board working together as a team for the common good of the library is one with which library directors readily identify. In my survey of 75 public library directors in the United States and Canada, this idea was a common thread in their responses concerning philosophies of dealing with a board of trustees.

AMENDMENTS

A final article in the board's bylaws should provide for the annual review and the process by which the bylaws may be amended. For example, the Anytown Library Board makes provision for change in article six as follows:

ARTICLE VI. REVIEW AND AMENDMENTS

The bylaws/goals committee of the library board shall review these bylaws annually and recommend changes to the board when a majority of the committee votes to do so. These bylaws may be amended at any regular meeting of the board with a quorum present, by majority vote of the members present, providing the amendment was stated in the call for the meeting.

This article of the Anytown Library Board makes the annual review of the bylaws a part of the bylaws/goals committee's responsibility. It states that the bylaws *must be reviewed* and also states the rules governing the actual amendment of the bylaws. In Anytown, if the bylaws are to be amended, the amendment will be discussed first in committee and then once more when it comes before the full board. It will not come as a surprise to any trustee because advance warning of the pending change must be given.

SUMMARY

State law and local ordinance give the library board its power and these provisions are usually incorporated into the board's bylaws. The board produces its own operating structure through a series of articles. These articles make up the bylaws under which the board and the library will operate. Bylaws are very important to the successful operation of any library board because they legalize the rules governing board function. Bylaws need to be reviewed annually both in committee and at a board meeting to make certain that they continue to offer the structure needed.

The library director's role in the formulation of board bylaws is often one of encouraging the board to take the lead. The board may be aided with examples of bylaws from other libraries, and may need to be reminded more than once to establish and review its bylaws. The actual writing of the bylaws is the board's responsibility.

ENDNOTES

1. Lynn M. Walding, Assistant Attorney General, "Opinion of the Attorney General Regarding a Proposed Ordinance of the Bloomfield, Iowa, City Council." pp. 1-2.

2. Ibid.

3. Ellis O. Butler, "Confessions of a Fusty Trustee" in *Tennessee Librarian* Volume 38, Number 1, Winter, 1986: 19.

4. Henry M. Martin, *Robert's Rules of Order*. New York: Scott Foresman, 1990.

5. Guy St. Clair and Joan Williamson, *Managing the One-Person Library*. London: Butterworth & Co. (Publishers) Ltd., 1986. p. 35.

2 LIBRARY TRUSTEES: PURPOSE & FUNCTION

The library director and the library board each play an important role in fulfilling the purpose and achieving the goals of the library for the community they serve. They must work in harmony to be effective.

A SHORT HISTORY

Library trustees have probably existed as long as libraries have. Scholars note that trustees served as early as 175 B.C. in Greece and Rome.[1] Monks in the middle ages had a supervisory role over the development of their monastary libraries, and examples of policies concerning hours of opening, care of materials, and security exist as part of the early history of what has evolved into the library board of trustees.[2]

In America as early as the eighteenth century, social libraries were developed by individuals who pooled books and donations of money to purchase books. These constituted a private library for the use of members. Lois K. Schochet notes: "The members of the social libraries elected permanent boards of trustees or directors to manage these institutions. While the conferred powers varied from board to board, they usually included the appointment, dismissal, and payment of officers and employees; the purchase of books, equipment and supplies; and occasionally the renting of buildings."[3]

Municipal tax-supported libraries became a reality in New England in the nineteenth century. An early example occurred in Connecticut where a privately established library for young people (the Bingham Library for Youth) was founded and placed under the control of a board of trustees. In 1810 citizens of the town voted to support the library with one hundred dollars for the purchase of books to add to the collection.[4] A few years later the first public library, supported from its inception by public monies, was established at Peterborough, New Hampshire. A board of three trustees was given the authority to formulate policies for this free public library open to everyone.[5]

Subsequently in Massachusetts, a state law was passed enabling towns to set up municipal public libraries. Initially two options were available: the library could be controlled by the city council, or it could establish its own board of trustees. The Boston Public Library was initially managed by a special committee of the city council, but later five citizens from the community were added. Legislative changes were made during the next few years which allowed the Library to be controlled by its own managing board, and this served as an example to other public libraries in the United States.[6] Complete control of the Library by the board was not reached until later, however. At first, the Boston City Council held the authority to appoint the librarian and fix his salary, but the trustees worked toward complete autonomy from the council, and full powers were eventually granted in 1878.[7]

Laws continued to be passed in the United States affecting public libraries and the way they were controlled. Some laws were brief and merely gave cities and towns the right to establish and fund libraries and to decide how they would be controlled. Other laws were more specific, going into great detail to legalize board control of the library.[8] The legal forms needed to establish public libraries and provide for library board jurisdiction varied from state to state and even from one size of library to another, yet a consistent pattern developed providing for a citizen board to oversee the development of the library. This same legislation enabled the board to appoint a librarian to administer the actual operation of the institution.[9]

Library boards maintained their authority to operate public libraries right into the twentieth century. The librarian, on the other hand, was often a mere custodian of the books, responsible only for loaning them out, seeing that they were returned, and collecting fines. The growth of the professional librarian's eventual responsibility for many aspects of the library and its development is a relatively recent phenomenon. The shift in authority from board to librarian became a necessity as library operations gradually became more complex. With an ever-increasing need for library administration, boards had no choice but to cede some of their absolute control of the library.[10] "Even in the early days of the Boston Public Library the librarian had surprisingly little authority. But as the tasks of administration increased in complexity, professionalization became necessary, and the membership at large and the governing boards were compelled to relinquish authority to the librarians."[11] Still, even today, some library boards—particularly in smaller towns where a professional librarian cannot be secured—continue to operate the library in the old manner, selecting the materials and employing all staff members, as well as formulating policies for library operation.

CONTROLLING BOARDS VS. ADVISORY BOARDS

The evolution of library boards in America has been toward increased control over the public library, but this trend appears to be reversing itself as city and town governments seek to regain their authority by eliminating the autonomous board, placing the library back under their direct control. When they are successful, the public library board becomes an advisory board. Its decisions are only suggestions which may be rejected by a higher authority. Advisory board members have less power than those of an administrative board, and since advisory boards are usually established by ordinance or resolution, their authority and even their existence can be easily challenged.[12] Advisory boards as yet make up only a small proportion of public library boards in the United States and Canada. Only 23 percent of the public libraries studied in my survey, taken in the spring of 1991, were advisory. Another 10 percent did not have library boards at all, but were controlled by municipal authority. The remaining 67 percent were controlled by fully empowered boards.

As this book was being written, the Iowa League of Municipalities, angered over one public library's refusal to disclose full financial data from its endowment fund, proposed legislation to the Iowa General Assembly which would give cities the power to eliminate public library boards without a referendum. The mere thought of eliminating library boards or even limiting their present authority brought about a storm of grassroots protest which, combined with efforts by the Iowa Library Association, defeated the bill in committee. This is an example, however, of the trend toward eliminating citizen boards which control public libraries.

An advisory board, with no authority or power to make the decisions which affect the public library, is obviously a weak board; advisory boards are often short-lived for this very reason. As members see their work and decisions consistently overruled by a city council, city manager, or other governmental authority with no understanding of the library's users, they abandon any hope of making real improvements and drop off the board. The board may eventually collapse under its own weight because members feel they can take no constructive action to better the library. This is not to say that advisory boards cannot serve a useful purpose for, even though they lack direct authority, they may still hold some influence over those who make decisions affecting the library.[13] Some library directors prefer to work with advisory boards, *because* they have no power. One library director in my survey suggested that when seeking a director's position, one should "pick an advisory board, not a governing board."

Purely advisory boards can create problems for the library director, however, because the situation may easily become one of serving two masters. The advisory board has no real authority yet it continues to advise the librarian, who must then answer to the government officials who make the final decisions regarding the library and its program. The library director is placed at the mercy of the local government, which rarely if ever accords a high priority to the library. Sooner or later this may become an unworkable situation and the demise of the advisory library board is probably the best outcome for all concerned and certainly for the eventual success of the library. My survey showed that 15 out of 16 library directors who worked with advisory library boards rated them as weak, unable to accomplish tasks, or easily obtain adequate funding for library operations.

The fact remains, however, that an effective board of citizens independent of municipal control is the best way to govern, support, and promote a public library. The people perceive the appointed or elected citizen library board as accountable to the taxpayers and in this way the community feels more in control, of its public library.[14]

PURPOSE OF THE LIBRARY BOARD

The broad purpose of any library board must be, first and foremost, to secure the best possible library it can for the community it serves. That should be the board's charge no matter what kind of library it serves—school, public, college, or university, or any one of a variety of special libraries. The board should constantly be seeking ways to fulfill its purpose, and this goal must guide everything the board does or attempts to do. The problem which often arises, however, is that even though the library board understands its purpose—the trustees have little or no understanding about how to achieve the goal.[15]

Trustees are responsible for the library's well-being. Their purpose will encompass decision making in at least five basic areas: "setting library policy, managing money, hiring and working with the librarian, carrying out public relations, and planning."[16] Intelligently thought-out decisions will result in effective policies which move the library toward excellence in all phases of operation and development.

FUNCTIONS OF THE DIRECTOR AND BOARD

The powers of the library board fall into six broad areas: providing for a building to facilitate library service; deciding on regulations for the use of the library; securing money for the operation of the library; contracting; creating financial operations; and establishing personnel policies and wage scales.[17] Without a doubt, the most important function of any library board is the hiring of the library director, for it is the director, working with the board, who will largely determine the success or failure of the library program. To these six broad areas, others may be added: long-range planning, public relations, and meeting and maintaining standards of library adequacy.

The common thread running through all of the board's powers is policy making, but not every trustee understands this role, or where policy ends and management begins. In the words of one trustee, "Policy should not be a rigid set of rules, but more of a blueprint or road map for library operations. Written policies let the public and staff know the library's position. They should be clearly written and understandable to all. Policy should be flexible and subject to change, with a regularly scheduled review to guarantee that it meets current situations."[18]

Problems can occur when the functions of the director and those of the library board are confused. Because the board's responsibilities are many and often include decisions which affect the actual operation of the library and its program, a misconception frequently develops that board and director functions overlap.[19] In reality, their functions are different, and it is essential to retain this difference if the two are to function responsibly and without friction. In the ideal sense, "the board does not (and should not) involve itself in the day-to-day operation of the library, and its public role, in all cases, should be one of support for the librarian and the work he is doing."[20]

My survey suggested that making a distinction between board functions and director functions was an immediate concern for most library directors. It was the most common concept verbalized by directors when asked for their general thoughts on working with library boards. A library director from Oregon put it this way: "Work with your board. Help them understand the difference between administrative responsibilities (yours) and policy-making responsibilities (theirs). Be candid with them, communicate with them, and they'll support you when you really need them."

Virginia Young has written a description of the parallel duties of directors and boards which should be made mandatory reading for every member of a library board. A copy should be placed in the hands of every new trustee *before* he or she begins a term on the library board:

DUTIES AND RESPONSIBILITIES

The library board and the library director may readily agree that the board deals with making policy while the director implements policy and manages the library. Still, trouble may occur because one or both fail to understand where policy ends and management begins.[22]

Crossover between library board duties and those of the library director can create serious problems and should be avoided. If it does happen, it is usually the result of a lack of communication. Crossing over is not always a one-way street, however. While one often thinks of the crossover as the board edging its way into the administration of the library, there is also the possibility of the library director usurping some of the powers and functions of the board. One of my Iowa colleagues told me that he rarely lets his board make important decisions on library matters! He asks for their opinions and makes the decisions himself. This procedure might be justified with an advisory library board, but is definitely wrong when dealing with a board (such as his) which has the legal authority to govern the library.

In either case a discussion of the difference between making policies (the board's function) and implementing those policies (the library director's function) is in order. A good time to call for such a discussion is at the annual meeting where officers of the board are elected. Sometimes a newly-elected board president, in an overzealous attempt to change the library, crosses the line and tries to implement board policies. A library director, on the other hand, may become so adept at anticipating the board that he strays into the policy-making function of the board, often without even realizing it. A discussion of the specific roles of the board and of the director will serve to reinforce the distinctions and create a feeling of harmony which leads to a constructive library program.

FIGURE 2-1   Duties and Responsibilities

Of the Library Board

1. Employ a competent and qualified librarian.

2. Determine and adopt written policies to govern the operation and program of the library.

3. Determine the purposes of the library and secure adequate funds to carry on the library's program.

4. Know the program and needs of the library in relation to the community; keep abreast of standards and library trends; cooperate with the librarian in planning the library program and support the librarian and staff in carrying it out.

5. Establish, support, and participate in a planned public relations program.

6. Assist in the preparation of the annual budget.

7. Know local and state laws; actively support library legislation in the state and nation.

8. Establish among the library policies those dealing with book and material selection.

9. Attend all board meetings and see that accurate records are kept on file at the library.

10. Attend regional, state, and national trustee meetings and workshops, and affiliate with the appropriate professional organizations.

11. Be aware of the services of the state library.

12. Report regularly to the governing officials and the general public.

Of the Librarian

1. Act as technical advisor to the board; recommend needed policies for board action; recommend employment of all personnel and supervise their work.

2. Carry out the policies of the library as adopted by the board.

3. Suggest and carry out plans for extending library services.

4. Prepare regular reports embodying the library's current progress and future needs; cooperate with board to plan and carry out the library program.

5. Maintain an active program of public relations.

6. Prepare an annual budget for the library in consultation with the board and give a current account of expenditures against the budget at each meeting.

7. Know local and state laws; actively support library legislation in the state and nation.

8. Select and order all books and other library materials.

9. Attend all board meetings other than those in which the librarian's salary or tenure are under discussion; may serve as secretary of the board.

10. Affiliate with the state and national professional organizations and attend professional meetings and workshops.

11. Make use of the services and consultants of the state library.

12. Report regularly to the library board, to the officials of local government, and to the general public.[21]

This is not to say that the library director does not have any say in formulating policies for the library, just that "a clear understanding of how the library administrator participates in policy making is prerequisite to successful management of library services."[23] Even though the library board's major responsibility is to adopt policy for all phases of operation, very few boards initiate their own policies. Policy recommendations usually come from the library director, for he or she is concerned with library management and knows which policies are needed.[24] In the words of a Wisconsin library director, "As chief executive officer of the library, the director must guide the board into its proper activity— policy-making. The development and review of policies that say what you really do is a very important task. If you don't think so, neither will your board. Make board meetings important policy- making or review meetings."

PREVENTING AN ADVERSARIAL RELATIONSHIP

An adversarial relationship can occasionally develop between the director and the board if they become alienated from each other, and it is the library and the community that will suffer the damage. Knowing the parallel functions of the two will help prevent such confrontations but, as any director who has stayed with the same library board for any length of time knows, some conflict may be inevitable. Too often, this conflict leads to the director resigning and taking a job in another community. This may be an advancement or merely a lateral move to avoid an unpleasant situation.

An established and competent library director who has served a community and improved the library to a state of comparative excellence may be able to resolve a conflict through compromise and communication, and without giving up any legitimate power in doing so. Likewise, a newly appointed director may be in a uniquely strong position with the board if there is a major conflict. For example, a professional librarian was hired in a small community where the library had previously been operated by a nonprofessional. When asked at the initial interview what she would do to improve the library, the new director had flatly stated that 90 percent of the adult nonfiction collection would have to be discarded because of its age and condition. One of the unwritten terms of her eventual employment agreement was that she would have the power to discard whatever materials from the collections she felt necessary. Two members of the library board, however, had second thoughts when she actually began to discard great quantities of books and a special meeting was called to discuss the problem. In this instance, the library director explained why it was necessary to discard so many books and reminded the board that it should not be a surprise to them since she had stated her collection improvement plans during the interview for the job. The board, faced with possible loss of their first professional librarian after only a few days on the job, agreed that she go ahead and continue to use her own discretion to weed the collection.

Communication is the key to defusing any adversarial relationship which develops between the board and the director. One of the problems in the field of librarianship is that it is sometimes too easy to abandon ship when conflict occurs. Disputes between board and director can be very unpleasant, and the temptation to go where one's abilities are appreciated is a very strong one, but it is better to stay and resolve the differences, if at all possible. There are dangers in leaving the position for both the director and the board. The director needs to learn the art of dealing effectively with the board because no matter where he or she goes, this will be a required basic skill. The board needs to work effectively with the director in order to improve the library in its community and will probably be unable to find a competent director if subservience and conflict is the rule. A director should only contemplate leaving a library and going on to a higher challenge when that director is riding a wave of success, not when things are going badly.

Impasses do develop between boards and library directors. In my survey, nearly 20 percent of the library directors who responded to the question indicated that at least once during their tenure as library directors they had found themselves in an untenable position with their boards; 50 percent of these indicated that they had backed down on the issue. Others compromised, sought out trustees individually, or resubmitted the question in a different form. One resigned and sought employment elsewhere.

A good working relationship between library board and library director must be established early on in the director's tenure. This relationship needs to be based "on open lines of communication and a high degree of mutual trust."[25] What is needed is a team concept with well-defined roles and responsibilities. Library improvement will be fostered only if the board and director cooperate with one another. As a library director from South Dakota stated: "Do not treat a board like an enemy, but provide them with ample information about the library and libraries in general—treat them as professionally as possible and don't be afraid to disagree with them in a rational, logical manner."

Complete honesty with the library board is essential in any conflict. If the library director's view about a problem is not communicated to the board accurately and fairly, an acceptable solution will probably not be forthcoming. A special meeting called to discuss a developing problem is the first step toward its eventual solution. It is important that everyone express an opinion in the matter—all members of the board and the director, not just one or two members of the board who have strong feelings.

SUMMARY

The purpose of any library board is to help produce the best possible library for the community it serves. It will achieve this goal if it works with the library director and does not allow a strained relationship to develop because of blurred roles. A team approach is essential in order to reach collective goals.

ENDNOTES

1. James Westfall Thompson, *Ancient Libraries*. Berkeley, CA: Archon Books, 1940. pp. 24-33.

2. Lois K. Schochet, "Historical Background," *Library Trends* 11, No. 10, July 1962: 5.

3. Schochet, pp. 6-7.

4. Jesse H. Shera, *Foundations of the Public Library*. Metuchen, NJ: Scarecrow Press Inc., 1965. pp. 158-159.

5. Shera, pp. 161-169.

6. Carleton Bruns Joeckel, *The Government of the American Public Library*. Chicago: University of Chicago Press, 1935. pp. 14-15.

7. Joeckel, pp. 16-22.

8. Joeckel, pp. 22-29.

9. Robert D. Leigh, *The Public Library in the United States*. New York: Columbia University Press, 1950. p. 111.

10. Shera, p. 108.

11. Donald J. Sager, *Managing the Public Library*. White Plains, NY, Knowledge Industry Publications Inc., 1984. p. 38.

12. Ellen Altman, ed. *Local Public Library Administration*. 2nd ed. Chicago: American Library Association, 1980. p. 29.

13. Alice B. Ihrig, *Decision Making for Public Libraries*. Hamden, CT: The Shoestring Press, 1989. p. 6.

14. Verna L. Pungitore, *Public Librarianship*. Westport, CT: Greenwood Press, 1989. pp. 52-53.

15. Diane J. Duca, *Nonprofit Boards: A Practical Guide to Roles, Responsibilities, and Performance*. Phoenix: The Oryx Press, 1986. p. x.

16. James Swan, "Inside the System: A Primer For Trustees." *Wilson Library Bulletin* 60, no. 6, February 1986: 28.

17. Sager, p. 38.

18. Swan, p. 28.

19. Robert D. Franklin, "The Administrator and the Board," *Library Trends*, 11, No. 1, July 1962: 56.

20. Guy St. Clair and Joan Williamson, *Managing the One-Person Library* London: Butterworth & Co. (Publishers) Ltd., 1986. p. 32.

21. Virginia G. Young, *The Trustee of a Small Public Library*. Chicago: American Library Association, 1978. p. 3.

22. Franklin, p. 56.

23. Altman, p. 33.

24. Pungitore, p. 56.

25. Ibid.

3 APPOINTMENT AND REMOVAL

A library board is ideally the extension of the people in the community which the library serves. The board should represent the interests of all parts of the community in order to function effectively. Trustees come to the board with both positive and negative perspectives, and it is the library director who faces the challenge of melding these viewpoints into a working board.

THE BOARD: DOES IT REPRESENT THE COMMUNITY?

One of the major failings of nearly all public library boards is that they do not accurately reflect their library's community. Library trustees tend to be selected from the same homogeneous pool of people, while often ignoring entire ethnic groups, socioeconomic classes, and age distinctions. The typical library trustee ranges in age from the middle years to elderly (often past retirement age); is usually a college graduate; has a comfortable income; is white, and is probably Protestant (or Catholic, if that is the dominant religion in the community). There is evidence to suggest that elected library boards are more representative of the population at large than are appointed boards.[1] Election to a library board may require residence in a specific district which, while not guaranteeing that the board will be more representative, may make it more likely.

The majority of public library trustees are appointed, however, not elected. My survey of public library directors in Canada and the United States found that 80 percent of the library boards were appointed boards. Of the remaining 20 percent, only ten public libraries had boards where all members were elected, and four had boards where only one of the trustees was elected and the others were appointed.

Perhaps somewhere there is a public library board that reflects the makeup of the community it serves. It would have a mix of trustees representing as many different factors in the community as possible. It would have blue-collar trustees and pink-collar trustees as well as professionals, businessmen, students, and *even* wives of doctors.[2] It would have persons who represent ethnic and religious minorities.[3] It would have a mix of ages including the young. It would have wealthy people, but it would also have people who do not have much money. In short, it would be a diverse group reflecting the diversity of the community. Library directors are keenly aware of this lack of diversity on their boards. When asked if they felt their library trustees were drawn from all facets of the community, the majority of surveyed directors stated that they did not feel that way.

Appointed library trustees are usually selected by a mayor or other government official. The library director and board may or may not have a hand in the selection process, and even when input is accepted, it is frequently ignored. Nevertheless, guidelines should be sent to the appointing authority whether they have been requested or not. The letter in Figure 3-1 was sent to the mayor of Anytown in an attempt to change the make-up of the library board so it would be more representative of the Anytown community. Note that the tone of the letter is advising, *not* demanding; these are merely suggestions. The mayor may ignore the letter completely or he may try to adjust his thinking in the appointment process to get some degree of balance on the library board.

A letter of this sort sent to the appointing authority may not have the immediate effect of making board appointments part of a well thought-out process, but it will probably improve appointments over the longer term. One of the difficulties with the process is that mayors and other officials who make appointments to the library board change frequently, and education must begin all over again with each new official.

I was surprised to learn from my survey that a majority of library directors felt that they had some input into the trustee selection process. Sixty-three percent indicated that they were regularly consulted when new trustees were to be appointed to the library board. Even more revealing was the fact that while a small majority (54 percent) of current boards discussed qualifications for new trustees and sent that information to those involved in the trustee selection process, nearly 79 percent sent names of people they felt would be good library trustees.

HOW TRUSTEES ARE APPOINTED

New trustees are appointed or elected to the library board under the regulations of the community they serve, but beyond that, how are trustees selected for the board before their appointment or election becomes official? Some may volunteer for the post. Several of my trustees became members by following this route. Many people who would like to become members of the library board

FIGURE 3-1   A Letter to the Mayor

Mayor John Walker
City Hall
Anytown, USA

Dear Mayor Walker:

It seems appropriate to write to you concerning future appointments
to the Anytown Public Library's Board of Trustees.

In order to function properly, the library board needs to be
representative of the community it serves and to achieve this goal we
need to strike a balance in a number of areas. Right now the board
consists of seven women and two men. We have found in the past
that a four/five split works better, and you may wish to consider this
when making your next few appointments.

Age is another factor, and at the present time nearly all of the
trustees are middle-aged. We need someone under thirty and
someone else past retirement age to represent the views of large
segments of the Anytown population. We have no one on the Board
who is handicapped nor anyone of a minority race, and these factors
too should be considered. A balance with regard to religion is also
desirable. I believe that right now we have eight Protestants and one
Catholic on the board, while a six to three ratio would be more
representative of the religious mix in our community. Finally, we
need some nonprofessionals as trustees. Too often, appointments
are made from the ranks of college graduates and other professional
people, but blue- and pink-collar workers use the library too, and
they need to have representation in order to make certain the board
adopts policies which reflect the will of *all* citizens in the community.

I trust that this will not complicate your selection of future trustees,
but I do hope that you will take these factors into consideration
before the next vacancy occurs. If I can be of any help to you in this
matter, please contact me.

Sincerely,

Sally Stevens, Library Director

don't seem to know how the appointment process works, and will contact the library director or another trustee and volunteer to be a board member. If this happens, they should be told about the proper procedure and asked to contact the person who makes the appointments. Elected library trustees will usually have more interest in the job than those who become library board trustees by appointment. In some instances they will have been persuaded to run by persons who hope to alter board policy for one reason or another. State law may require that library board members run for election. This is true for regional library trustees in Iowa. The law is based on the assumption that elected trustees will be more responsive to the will of the people.[4]

All too often, appointment to the library board is rooted in politics. For example, one of my most avid library users and supporters volunteered to serve on the library board. She had moved to our city from a larger metropolitan area, and had used our library heavily from the first day she and her family arrived. At that time, our library was in the early stages of an extensive collection rebuilding program, and had lost many of our users due to inadequacies in the collections. This new arrival, recognizing that a change was being made, talked up the library to anyone who would listen throughout the town. She was active in the community, joined the friends of the library group, and eventually served as its president. Numerous people spoke to the mayor about her appointment to the library board, but vacancy after vacancy occurred and she was never asked. A former library trustee took it upon himself to uncover the reason, and he discovered that it was because her husband had sought a seat on the city council when the family first moved to town. The mayor looked upon him as an upstart who had no business running against the incumbent and, apparently to teach him a lesson, would not appoint his wife or any member of his family to any city board. Politics prevented a potentially good library trustee from being appointed to a position where she could help the library. It took two changes of mayors before she was finally appointed to the library board, where she served with distinction.

While some appointed trustees are enthusiastic volunteers, others are appointed to the library board as a reward or favor. Still others receive appointment because they have complained about the library. One of my best trustees became a library board member because he was continually complaining to the mayor and city council about nearly every aspect of library operation. He came to the library board as a new trustee at my first meeting with the board and was an effective supporter for library progress for many years. Another trustee was appointed because he wanted the library open on Sundays—a change he eventually persuaded the board to adopt. Others who have openly opposed increases in the library's budget have been appointed to the library board at times when city officials have been less supportive of the library program.

In some communities the library board and library director may have a direct hand in appointments to the board. Having served as director of the same public library for 28 years, I have seen all variations on the appointment theme, from mayors who would die before they would appoint anyone *I* suggested to those who sought me out and asked me to suggest possible appointees. Having a hand in the appointment process does not always turn out well, however. Once I suggested someone I felt would be an outstanding trustee only to find, after his appointment, that he was an ineffective decision maker and often sided with with the mayor against the library!

Whether or not to take an active role in the trustee selection process is a decision each library director will have to make. I like to think that I can work with any person who is appointed to my board and in nearly all instances this is true, but there are times when the library director is asked to help select new trustees. It is best to suggest several names for appointment instead of just one name. That allows the person who makes the appointment more latitude and he or she feels comfortable because a choice between candidates is made.

SECURING CONSTRUCTIVE BOARD MEMBERS

Library trustees are representatives of the community and they play an important role in the development of a good library. It is of great importance that effective lay people are placed on the library board.[5]

One of the most helpful ways I have found to secure good members for the library board has been to first "try them out" on the executive board of the friends of the library. It is an almost ideal proving ground for future library trustees not just because it gives the director the opportnity to measure commitment to the library, but also because one can gain insight into the effectiveness of potential library trustees in a board situation. People differ in their abilities to deal with one another constructively and it can become very obvious in a friends board setting exactly who has the necessary skills to work effectively with other people and who does not.

Current members of the library board are often knowledgeable about possible new trustees, and can be brought into the selection process. The director must recognize, however, that there is the danger that members may want their friends to serve on the board regardless of their abilities. Another problem is that board members often recommend candidates from out of their own segment of the community and you may end up with new trustees who are carbon copies of those already serving on the board. This may do wonders for unity and cohesiveness, but it may also result in a lack of new ideas and an absence of culturally diverse viewpoints.

The size of the library board will vary from library to library. In my survey I found two library boards which had memberships of only three trustees. At the other extreme, one library board had 25 members. The most common number of library trustees serving a public library was five members, with seven members a close second.

Some library boards seek to fill certain roles on the board in an effort to increase board expertise in a variety of areas. The larger the board, the more likely it is that such a practice will be successful. It has been suggested that library boards have in their membership men and women who are experts in accounting, law, education, public relations, and library and information science.[6] This can cause a problem because the "experts" may feel so well-qualified that they go beyond their roles as policy makers and dabble in library management as well. Another danger in this practice is that these so-called "experts" all come from the same library trustee pattern: college graduates. By adding them to the library board we continue to perpetuate a board that does not represent the community served by the library.

If the appointing authorities request a list of names to choose from, it is better for the current library trustees to provide one, even though it may contain a certain amount of bias, than to trust providence to yield a good trustee. It is important when discussing names to go on such a list, however, to seek all types of people represented by the community: the old and the young, men and women, professionals and nonprofessionals, college graduates and noncollege graduates, and cultural and ethnic minorities of all kinds. Getting the list to the proper authorities is easy if it has been requested, but even if it hasn't been one can still be provided. It may be used or it may be ignored, but at least the idea will have been planted that there are people in the community who would be good library trustees. It is unwise, however, to contact the people on your list prematurely. Unless you can actually offer them an appointment, asking them if they would be willing might give them false hope for an appointment which may, for whatever reason, never come.

One of the misconceptions I often hear from other librarians is that the "good trustee" is one who uses the library. This is not always true. Some of my best trustees have been those who entered the library only for board meetings, and some of my worst have been avid users of the library. The critical factor in the success or failure of a library board is the *power* members hold—not just the power given them as a board by the state, but the power they have in the community from *before* they became library trustees.

The board that hired me, for example, was a power board. It consisted of nine trustees, the majority of whom were very powerful in the community. We had a prominent lawyer who also served as county attorney, the owner and publisher of the only daily newspaper in a five-county region, the town's wealthiest man (a retired rancher), the wife of a banker, a dentist who would later serve on the city council, and two women who were very active in community matters. The other two were well-known, but relatively outside of the power structure. Of the group, only one was an occasional reader and user of the library, and only three had library cards, but the library achieved more during their tenure than at any other point in its history because they effectively used their power to pave the way for change. They increased the book budget by 500 percent the second year I was library director, and it became the highest per capita materials budget in the state. They encouraged me to develop a long-range plan for the library. Notice was served that a new library building was needed. A friends of the library group was started, shelving was expanded, new furniture purchased; in short, it was an active and powerful board, but none of its members were regular library users.

Some of the weaker boards I have served with have been those on which active library users made up a majority of the library board. They loved the library and all seemed to have a strong stake in making program and collection improvements, but they were ineffective because they had no raw power to force the changes through the political structure of the city and county governments. Most library improvements require money, and unless the library has a large endowment fund, the funds will have to come from the taxes which provide most of the library's support. Unless the library board is powerful in its often behind-the-scenes dealings, the money probably won't be there to support the library. I often tell my board that it's not just the library director who makes the library a good one, it is also the board's ability to raise the needed funds for change which will mean the difference between an excellent library and a mediocre one.

HOW TRUSTEES ARE REMOVED

Trustees are appointed to library boards for a variety of reasons and these reasons may not always be positive ones. Trustees with an axe to grind may try to sabotage the library program and attempts at changing and improving it. Removal of trustees is a delicate matter. Generally, there are only two legitimate reasons for removal and these reasons are spelled out in the library's bylaws (and often in the city code as well.) Failure to attend a specified number of board meetings is the first reason for removal, and moving from the district is the other. But what happens when an appointed library trustee is truly against the library and seeks only to halt library improvements for whatever reason—be it antagonism toward the library director, a wish to keep property taxes down, or something entirely different?

Perhaps the first course of action is to attempt to change the trustee's attitude into a positive one. There was one trustee early in my career who was downright surly at board meetings. She very obviously had a couple of drinks before each meeting and invariably opposed most of my ideas for improving the library. Although the other trustees were willing to go along with me and approve all but my most outlandish proposals, this woman consistently voted against them and, even worse, she seemed to despise me personally. I worried about her behavior and tried to figure out what I had done to get on her wrong side from the very beginning, but I could not figure her out. I began to seek out her opinion on nearly every matter at board meetings, and she seemed to thaw out a bit. It finally occurred to me that because the previous librarian had not been a professional and had relied on the board to do much of the administration of the library, perhaps this trustee resented the fact that I had taken full charge of management and relegated the board to its true role of policy maker. I began looking for opportunities to test my theory and to work her back into the fabric of library improvement. She seemed to have a natural flair for interior decoration and so, when it became time to choose the colors and decor of the new building, I boldly suggested at a board meeting that she work with the architect on this matter instead of me, hinting that I really didn't have much sense about these things. The change in her attitude and behavior was instantaneous. Overnight she became one of the library's strongest supporters and eventually my good friend as well. I was fortunate to have understood the antagonism she must have felt when I took over as director, but it took me nearly ten years to figure out the problem and arrive at a solution!

I was not so lucky with another trustee who made it very plain at my first board meeting that he felt city taxes in general, and taxes to support the library in particular, were too high and he did not want them increased for any reason. Throughout the nearly 20 years he served as a library trustee we were adversaries. He always questioned any bill over $100 and opposed all increases in the library's funding unless they came from funds not generated by the 29 properties he owned (a fact he managed to mention at nearly every meeting.) Reports and proposals showed that because of the money the library was receiving, we were able to better serve the people of the community and that use of the library was forever increasing, but all this was to no avail. He attended every meeting and was outspokenly critical of all library expenses, especially salary increases. His cries were heard patiently by other members of the board and then ignored—making his voice a disruptive one, but not one that actually affected the progress of the library. Some trustees will always be negative no matter what you do, and you will just have to learn to tolerate and work around them.

There are ways to remove antagonistic trustees from the library board, but it is best that the library director not take an active role in trustee removal. One of my early trustees was a rare combination in that she was powerful in city government circles and could influence people on the library's behalf if she chose to do so. Her husband and family were heavy users of the library and seemed to appreciate the improvements that were being made. Sadly enough, however, this trustee, who came on the board a few years after I was hired, seemed to be goading me into resigning from my position as library director. Everything I was for, she was against, and she seemed to enjoy ridiculing me at board meetings. She was not without influence with other trustees, and she was ultimately elected president of the library board.

Efforts to change her behavior did not succeed and after considering my position I began looking for another job. It was obvious that this was a personal matter and one that was not going to go away. I was interviewed for a more responsible position at a county-wide system in my home state and was considering making a move if the job was offered. In the meantime, I attended a party at a friend's house and was asked by a former library trustee how things were going with the library board. Without thinking, I mentioned that I was looking for another job because the board president and I weren't getting along and that she opposed every improvement I suggested for the Library. We didn't talk about it very long and soon went on to other topics and I never gave our conversation another thought—at least not until three days later when I read on the front page of the local newspaper that the president of the library board had "resigned to pursue other interests." I was stunned because I knew that my remarks at the party had caused her dismissal from the board.

Even though the difficulty was resolved and I was able to stay and continue to improve the library, I always felt guilty about my inadvertent role in the solution. At the same time, however, I was pleased that those in charge of city government were so committed to improvement of the library that they would take action to remove a trustee who impeded this progress. A library director from Georgia had a similar situation on her board—a trustee who was continually antagonistic. The problem was resolved by other members of the library board who talked the trustee into resigning.

A more certain answer to the problem of difficult and negative trustees on the board is to limit their terms of office by statute. In some public libraries, trustees tend to serve forever and often have to die in order to be released from membership on the board. The governing authority can and *should* pass an ordinance limiting the number of consecutive terms a library trustee can serve. If such a statute cannot be arranged, the library board may wish to make it a part of its own bylaws.[7] In this way the board will have a turnover of talent and will also propel ex-trustees out into the community, without hard feelings, where many will still support the library. There is such a thing as "board fatigue" resulting in library trustees becoming less effective, often without even realizing it themselves, because the board has become stagnated due to a lack of new trustees and corresponding new ideas.[8]

The survey showed that while most terms for library board members are limited by statute or bylaws or both, more than a third of the library directors who responded stated that there was no limit on the number of terms library trustees could serve. For the majority where trustee terms are limited, the limits varied widely from a low of two years on the board to a high of sixteen years.

Of course, in addition to the few trustees you don't mind losing, there will be those dedicated individuals who have supported you and the library program. It will be hard to let them go. But the fact remains that library boards can become stale when the same trustees serve year after year. "After about eight or ten years on a board, individuals become too familiar with the organization and can become annoyed hearing the same old problems come up over and over again."[9]

Another problem is created when the new rule goes into effect. There could be an almost immediate changing of the guard, as trustees' terms expire and new trustees take their places. It can be very disrupting to change the entire board in a matter of a few short years because the continuity between the old and the new can be lost, so careful attention should be given to staggered terms during the transition period. "The value of the experienced board member lies with the understanding and knowledge of the organization that comes with tenure."[10] If the local government does not limit terms on the library board, and the board of trustees resists such a change in its bylaws, it is within bounds for the library director to suggest such a change to the appropriate government authorities. Limiting terms by statute is more effective than doing so with board bylaws, for the latter are not always followed in every instance.

THE PERFECT TRUSTEE

The perfect trustee doesn't exist—at least I haven't encountered one yet! I want someone who is as interested in the library as I am, but one who will stick to the role of policy maker and not stray over into my job as library administrator. I want someone who is willing to be an advocate for the public library in the community and who will work with state legislators for positive library laws and funding. Trustees should have constructive ideas and should relay input from citizens about the local library. I want powerful trustees who use their influence to make substantial gains for the library, its collections, and programs. I want trustees who attend every meeting of the board because they want to, not because they have to. I want creative people who don't mind stating their opinion on everything even though it may be different from mine. I want someone who wants the public library to be the focal point of the community and will help to achieve that goal. I want trustees who are open-minded and fair and who will listen to all sides of arguments and make their own decisions. I want library trustees who want the best possible library we can have for the people we serve!

THE CHANGING BOARD

Every time a new trustee is appointed or elected to the board, there will be a change in that board. Not just because the new trustee brings a different outlook and mind-set to the group, but also because the board loses an old member who has over the years become an educated and perhaps valuable trustee. The change may be minor or major, but *it will be a change.* Many new trustees don't feel comfortable on the board until they have served at least one year; others, sensing that maybe they don't really belong (perhaps they are not made from the same mold as other trustees), may never become wholly comfortable. Few new trustees, in my experience, have had more than a vague awareness of the board's role in the operation of the community library. One of my new trustees was astounded to learn that the board actually controlled a budget for library services!

The library director should aid in the integration process by helping the new trustee become acclimated to the library board. One way to do this is to visit with the new trustee prior to the first meeting. The new library board member needs to know how the board functions, what types of business it deals with, how the trustees operate within the board's structure, the differences between the trustees' role and that of the administrator, and the names of current library trustees.

The library director may wish to give the new trustee a guided tour of the library building at this time. Just a visit is not enough, however. The new trustee needs to be provided with a copy of the board's bylaws, all library policies adopted by the board, the annual report of the library, recent reports of the library director, and the minutes of previous board meetings. Usually about a year's worth of this sort of information will be helpful to the newly appointed or elected trustee. It is also a good idea at this time to give the new trustee a copy of "Duties and responsibilities of the library board and of the librarian."[11] It is the library director's obligation to orient the new trustee to the board before his or her first meeting. Failure to do so will inevitably mean a difficult transition from lay person to library trustee, and will often have far-reaching negative effects on the library and its programs.

SUMMARY
It is of the utmost importance to find library trustees who are capable, intelligent, and willing to work cooperatively with the library director to improve the library. Trustees should represent as many facets of the community as possible in order to present a diversity of ideas for library development. Powerful library boards can raise the adequacy of libraries in the communities they serve.

ENDNOTES

1. Mary E. Arney "Library Boards—Who They Are and How They Get There," *Show-Me Libraries* Spring 1988: 24.

2. The Carroll, Iowa, Public Library is a typical example of a library board that does not accurately represent and reflect the composition of people in the community it serves. Over the past 25 years it has had 29 different trustees serve on its library board. Eleven were in the medical profession or related to a medical person; ten were in business; three were lawyers or wives of lawyers; three were bankers; and two were teachers. Only one was not a college graduate, and only one represented a minority ethnic group (the most recent appointee). City ordinance dictates that one member of the board be selected from the rural community, but a farmer has never been appointed— instead, a professional person from the same mold as the other trustees has always been chosen (first a dentist and later a teacher). All have been middle-aged or older with not a single trustee ever serving on the board who was under 30. Religious affiliation has often been unbalanced, and a disabled person has never been appointed despite the fact that there are many in the community.

3. Arney, p. 24.

4. Verna L. Pungitore, *Public Librarianship*. Westport, CT: Greenwood Press, 1989. p. 51.

5. Jean T. Kreamer, "The Library Trustee as a Library Activist," *Public Libraries*, 29, No. 4, July/August 1990: 221.

6. Diane J. Duca, *Nonprofit Boards: A Practical Guide to Roles, Responsibilities, and Performance*. Phoenix, AZ: The Oryx Press, 1986. p. 150.

7. Duca, p. 150.

8. Ibid.

9. Virginia G. Young, *The Trustee of a Small Public Library*. Chicago: American Library Association, 1978. p. 3.

10. Ed Klee, "The Public Library Board is Looking for a Few Good Trustees," *Kentucky Libraries,* Winter 1989: 18-21.

11. Kreamer, p. 220.

4 STANDING AND SPECIAL COMMITTEES

A library board will need to have standing committees to help simplify board activities by laying the groundwork for effective decisions and their resulting policies. Standing committees divide up the areas of board jurisdiction and meet periodically to discuss and recommend policies in the various areas of library operation and development. Special committees may be appointed to solve problems of limited duration. The library director must be able to work with committee members if the library is to achieve excellence.

Depending upon the size of the board, committees can serve a valuable purpose and strengthen the ability of the board to operate in an effective manner. If the board is small (five members or less) dividing into committees would be a waste of time and the board might better act as a whole, making policy decisions as a group rather than depending upon a structure of committees to make recommendations to the full board. When the board consists of seven members or more, however, committees can be extremely useful by studying individual problems and bringing their ideas and conclusions to the full board, where the final decisions are made. Studies have shown that the larger the group, the more time is required to reach decisions.[1] Effective committees can help reduce the time needed in the decision-making process. "The use of committees to accomplish organizational objectives is based on the premise that smaller groups of individuals can conduct themselves more efficiently than the whole and that a definitive structure is required to operate efficiently."[2] Only a little more than a third of the public library directors in the United States and Canada covered by my survey indicated that their library boards operated with a system of standing and special committees.

COMMITTEE STRUCTURE

Large library boards operate most effectively when divided into committees. The committee is charged with doing the groundwork and research in a typical area of concern for library policy and making recommendations on that policy to the full board. Committees commonly are made up of at least three members and may include more depending, of course, upon the size of the board. But just as a board can become unwieldy by being too large, a committee can also suffer from the same problem.

The committee structure is established by the bylaws of the

library board which will state which committees the board will have, the number of members on each, where the members will come from (whether they need to be strictly from the parent board or if outsiders may also serve), the areas of policy to be studied by each, and the frequency with which particular committees will meet. Committees are appointed by the president of the board, who will also designate one member as committee chairperson. The wise board president will take into consideration the preferences of each board member regarding the committee on which they wish to serve. However, committee assignments should be changed periodically so that stagnation does not occur and new ideas are brought in by other members. The library director is a nonvoting member of each committee and attends all meetings. The president of the board may also wish to attend committee meetings and needs to be notified about them.

TYPES OF COMMITTEES

Standing committees are those with functions required for the proper operation of the board. Typical standing committees include a *ways and means committee* to deal with financial matters such as the annual budget, fees for nonresidents, personnel policies, and salaries and wages; an *operations committee* to deal with policies on the day-to-day operation of the library including building and grounds, hours of opening, charges for lost and overdue materials, library cooperation and extension, and services to schools and other groups; and a *bylaws/goals committee* for board bylaws, book selection policies, memorials and gifts, and long-range planning. Some public library boards split personnel policies off from the ways and means committee into a *personnel committee.*

The number and type of standing committees will vary from library to library. Larger libraries may want more committees, but the smaller library will usually be able to manage effectively with just three standing committees. In my survey of public library directors 21 different committees were cited. The most common ones (named by the most directors) were finance, building and grounds, and personnel.

Special committees may be appointed by the board president at any time for any purpose beyond the established jurisdictions of the standing committees. The Anytown Public Library, for example, has three special committees in addition to its three standing committees: the *Materials Review Committee,* which functions only when a citizen from Anytown's service area challenges the library's right to have a specific piece of material on its shelves; the *Public Relations Committee,* which plans special events promoting the library above and beyond the regular media stories written by the library staff; and the *Fine Arts Committee,* which organizes art shows at the library on a time-to-time basis. One advantage of special committees is that expertise not available on the board can be drawn from the community at large. Thus the Anytown Library Board's Fine Arts Committee is chaired by a library trustee, but also includes two interested people from the community. Another example of a special committee is one appointed to choose a new library director. This *search committee* may meet frequently over a short period of time (until the new director is hired) and then cease to function.

Committees only have the power to recommend, not the power to act as separate entities. Both standing and special committees function as subdivisions of the library board and may make recommendations, but not establish library board policy.

The committee structure of the library board is useful to ease the transition from lay person to library trustee. Membership on the larger board of trustees can often be an intimidating experience. In the smaller community, many of the trustees currently serving on the library board are familiar but the new appointee may not have worked with them on other boards or in the community. In larger communities, many of the existing trustees will be complete strangers. The new trustee will probably not have a working knowledge of the functioning library board. Library board meetings are not always reported in the newspaper and they may be largely a mystery to the uninitiated. New trustees have often told me that they were totally unaware of "what it was, exactly, that the library board did," and even after reading the bylaws and perusing the minutes of past meetings they were hazy about what to expect at their first board meeting. Because the board is often large and filled with seemingly knowledgeable men and women who understand how the board operates and what is expected of them, the new trustee can best be integrated onto the board through the committee structure.

In Anytown, as in many others, only the Ways and Means Committee meets more than once a year, so the chances of a new trustee meeting with a committee before a first board meeting are slim. New trustees tend to be relatively silent at the first few meetings. A skillful board president will ask the opinion of the new trustee on various matters. Indeed, the new trustee is in a unique and valuable position during early board and committee meetings because he or she views library policy from a somewhat different angle, and can make cogent observations as an outsider. At the first board meeting, the newly appointed trustee should be placed on one of the standing committees and told when it will meet and which areas of board policy it will study.

SMALL GROUP PSYCHOLOGY

Smaller groups, like library board committees, offer greater opportunity for expression and participation because they *are* small. It is very difficult, if not impossible, to be a member of a three-person committee meeting and not voice one's opinion on the matters being discussed. For this reason, the committee is a good way to integrate a new trustee into the ebb and flow of board structure. By meeting with a small number of library trustees, the new member becomes better acquainted with the others and this will prove helpful at future board meetings.

The chair of the committee is in the relatively powerful position of being able to steer the direction of committee discussion, but can be overruled by other committee members. The committee must contain an odd number of members to insure that votes do not end in ties. The library director and the board president attend the committee meetings and have input into the discussion, but do not have a vote on recommendations to make to the full board.

The size of the committee will depend, in part, on the size of the parent board and the number of committees. Each library trustee should serve on at least one committee. No one should be left out of the committee structure. As the committee size increases, the effectiveness of the group decreases, as does the likelihood that all members will not have their say. ". . .Smaller groups are more efficient, and they work better than a large committee. It's easier to assign responsibility for action, to follow up and judge results, and get things done. The larger the group, the greater the tendency to avoid taking action, to speak in generalities, and to fail in the important follow-up actions that decisions demand."[3]

COMMITTEE MEETINGS

Advance notice of all committee meetings should be made to the members of the committee, the library director, the president of the library board, and the media. The library director often serves as secretary of the board and of the committees and will send out the notices and take the minutes of the meeting. Notice of the meeting should be mailed at least one week before the scheduled meeting. An agenda and any pertinent reports or background information should be sent to committee members a few days before the meeting. If such data is sent too early, it may be set aside and forgotten by the date of the meeting. If it is important to bring this material to the meeting it should be so stated when it is sent out. Even so, it is a good idea to have extra copies available in case committee members forget to bring their material.

Committee members should decide where they wish to meet, what time is most convenient, and agree on a date which is good for everyone. The committees of the Anytown Public Library Board decided long ago that it would be most convenient to hold luncheon meetings. This was the time when most working trustees could get together during the day, so they agreed to meet at noon at one of the local restaurants. No attempt is made to keep these meetings private or secret, no matter what the topic under consideration. The committee meeting, like the parent library board meeting, should be held in public. Thus the Anytown committees meet at a table in the main dining room within earshot of anyone present. Since notice of the meeting is released to the newspapers and radio station, the public is free to attend—though no one in Anytown has ever done so except for an occasional newspaper reporter.

"A committee structure is effective when several elements are present. First, it is imperative that all committees have definite tasks. Second, committee chairpersons must be capable of leading committee members through a rational decision-making process in order to reach appropriate decisions. Third, each committee should include at least one key program director or manager from the organization's staff. Fourth, members must be willing to give whatever time is required to their fact-finding, evaluation, or other activities. Last, committees must conduct their business in a timely fashion. A decision or recommendation stalled in committee can destroy an important timetable for the organization."[4] The committee must be task-oriented in order to function effectively. When the committee has been instructed to meet by the parent library board, the purpose of the meeting must be spelled out in definite terms. When the charge to the committee is vague, the committee—unsure of its exact purpose—will probably not reach a germane recommendation for the board to consider.

There is a certain amount of groundwork which must be done prior to any committee meeting. Generally, the preparation for the meeting is accomplished by the library director. On sensitive issues like staff salaries, the information may be gathered by a committee member. If the committee does not have all of the correct and relevant facts when it meets, its decisions and recommendations will be faulty. "Effective discussion grows out of dependable knowledge and clear thinking, which can only come from preparation."[5]

In order for the board to function responsibly, the committees will have to do a conscientious and thorough job. Not only will their research and careful consideration of the problem need to be complete, but they must also be able to make a positive recommendation to the board. "Much of the action taken by a board emanates from its. . .committee meetings. If these meetings are ineffective, it follows that the work of the board may also be ineffective."[6] Just as with the full board, the effectiveness of the committee will depend in large measure on the ability of the committee chair to lead the discussion and direct it in such a way that the committee members reach a quality decision. A chair who allows the discussion in committee to wander away from the problem at hand will do a disservice to the library board, for the decisions made by the committee will likely be poor ones.

To illustrate the workings of the committee structure we may look at a typical meeting of the Anytown Public Library Board's Operations Committee when it discussed the request from a citizen's group to expand the Library's hours. A petition signed by 50 people had been presented at the last board meeting which demanded that the Anytown Public Library open at nine o'clock each morning and remain open until ten o'clock each evening. The board had discussed the petition briefly and then voted to refer the issue to the Operations Committee for further study and recommendations.

Committee members remained after the board meeting was adjourned to discuss what information needed to be gathered before the committee met. Cost figures would be very important so the library director was asked to compile these figures based on full library service for the extended hours. Other required information included an analysis of the signatures on the petition: who were these people, how many had current library cards at the Anytown Library, how many were not able to get to the Library during the present hours schedule, and how many could be expected to use the Library if the new hours were adopted? Analysis would be made also of library hours in other communities of Anytown's size. The library director was asked to write a report covering these factors and any others deemed important, and to send a copy of the findings to each member of the committee prior to the committee meeting.

The library director gathered the information and put it all into a report which was then distributed to the committee members. Note that this was to be just a factual report. The committee did not ask for the director's recommendation. It is important for the person compiling the background information not to inject value judgements concerning the matter.

When the committee met, they had all had an opportunity to read through the report and formulate questions about the present library hours and the citizens' request for change. They knew how much it would cost the Anytown Public Library per hour per year to implement the changes and they knew whether or not the necessary funds were available in the current operating budget. They had been informed as to who was making the demands for change, not by name, but by characteristic (how many had library cards, how many were actually now prevented from using the library because of its hours, how many could be expected to use the new hours, as well as population statistics of age, sex, occupation, etc.) The committee members knew what the open hours were at other public libraries in communities Anytown's size.

It turned out that nearly all of the people who signed the petition were students at the local community college and were reacting to a restriction of library hours at their community college due to financial cutbacks. In short, members of the Operations Committee had all of the facts they needed to make an intelligent and informed decision about the request for increased open hours. After a discussion, the committee decided to recommend to the library board that the hours be partially modified, within budget limitations, to accommodate the students. The library director wrote up the minutes of the meeting and sent copies to each member of the committee, including those who were absent from the meeting. It is very important to keep *all* members of the committee informed, not just those who are able to attend the meeting. An informed committee will be a more responsive committee, and one cannot ignore members just because they are unable to make it to all the meetings.

THE LIBRARY DIRECTOR'S ROLE

The library director should always take a neutral stance at committee meetings, even though he or she has an opinion and feeling about nearly every policy matter taken up in committee. The facts on all sides of the problem must be fairly presented whatever the director's own viewpoint. Remember that the committee discussion and recommendations are part of the process of policy making, the true function of the library board. The library director acts as a technical expert marshalling the facts for free discussion by committee members. This is not to say that the library director cannot make suggestions and recommendations to the committee and the board, but that these recommendations based on expertise and management experience need to be made *after* discussion and founded on factual information made available to both the committee and the board. The committee may specifically request the director's recommendations and then, of course, these will become a part of the report. This is fine as long as it is labeled as the director's recommendation and not construed as factual information. For example, at the Anytown Public Library, the Ways and Means Committee specifies that on matters of wage and salary increases, the library director shall make recommendations for each library employee including himself or herself in a report to the committee at its budget meeting. The director makes recommendations when asked to do so but, for most committee discussions, it is better not to make a recommendation until after committee members have thoroughly talked about the topic under study.

PRESENTING RECOMMENDATIONS

Once the committee decides on its recommendations to the full board, it is up to the director to put these recommendations into an acceptable form for the chair to present at the board meeting. Data gathered for the committee should be summarized to show the trustees that the committee has done its homework before making its decisions. It is not necessary to provide the board with the same full factual report prepared for the committee. Copies of the report used by the committee may be available at the board meeting should other trustees dispute the recommendations and wish to have more detail. The recommendation to the board is best if kept brief and to the point—one page if possible. An introductory paragraph refreshes the memories of the trustees about the problem:

Recommendations Concerning the Library's Hours of Opening.

Introduction: At the March 10, 1991 meeting of the Anytown Public Library's Board of Trustees a petition of 50 names was presented asking the library board to consider a change in hours so that the library would open each day at nine a.m. and close at ten p.m. The library board discussed the matter and voted to refer it to the Operations Committee for study and recommendations.

The next paragraph summarizes the information gathered for the committee:

Background Information: The Operations Committee asked the library director to gather data about the request, which showed that 48 of the signatures on the petition were those of students at Anytown Community College. Contact with the librarian at the college ascertained that the community college library was having to shorten its hours of opening due to a cutback in funding. The Anytown Community College library will no longer be open evenings effective April 1, 1991. Thirty signers of the petition have active cards at the Anytown Public Library, 20 do not.

The Anytown Public Library is currently open from 10:00 a.m. until 8:00 p.m. on weekdays and from 10:00 a.m. until 6:00 p.m. on Saturdays.[7] In order to provide full service during the added hours requested in the petition, the library would need to be staffed with a professional librarian, a library clerk, and a library page for 19 additional hours per week. The cost to the Anytown Public Library for these hours in terms of salaries, wages, benefits, heating, cooling, and lighting would amount to approximately $35 per hour or a total of $665 per week. The projected cost to the library for these additional hours for one year is $34,580. The Anytown

Public Library does not have funds available in its current operating budget to fund this added expense.

The Operations Committee met at noon on March 17, 1991 to discuss the report. One member of the committee became ill and was not able to attend this meeting, but both the president of the board and the library director were present.[8]

The final section gives the operations committee recommendations and the reasons for these recommendations:

Recommended Action: The committee recommends that the Anytown Public Library remain open until nine o'clock on weekday evenings during the months September through June.

It was the consensus of the committee that the problem was primarily that of the Anytown Community College, not the Anytown Public Library. Though a majority of the people whose names appear on the petition use the public library, the committee members felt that that was no guarantee they would use the public library during all of the additional hours requested. The college library is open during the morning hours so the public library would not need to be open for students during those times. The committee agreed that increasing the hours to a nine o'clock closing time on weekdays during the school year would be one way of accomodating the students, and would benefit all members of the Anytown Community and lead to increased library use.

Committee meetings, like library board meetings, do not always run smoothly. Most library boards contain at least one continually negative trustee and some contain several! These members cannot be excluded from the committee structure any more than they can be excluded from the library board, and they most definitely can cause problems. Once again, the board president will know who these individuals are and can reduce the chances for conflict by making careful appointments. Some of the committees of a library board are more critical to the successful operation of the library than others and negative trustees can be shunted to the less important committees where their ideas will have less impact. Another ploy which often works is to place a negative trustee on a committee with several others who are very pro-library. In this way unconstructive ideas are aired, but effectively smothered by the others.

This is not to imply that dissent is not a valuable part of any decision-making process. In order for a committee to meet its obligations and reach meaningful recommendations for the full board, views contrary to those of the majority are very important and may often lead to positive solutions which might otherwise not have been considered.[9] An Illinois library director summed it up in the following way way when referring to trustees and the advice is appropriate both in committee meetings and at meetings of the full board: "Respect them. Remember they are individuals, not a single entity." Stress the "importance of working for common understanding and consensus to the degree possible. The rubber stamp situation is *not* an ideal to be sought. The best situation is if each individual thinks through issues and speaks his/her mind."

In my experience with library board committees, only very rarely does the committee's recommendation get "shot down" at the board meeting. Because the committee can go into the matter in detail and discuss many of the possible repercussions of their recommendations, members of the committee come to the board meeting with a distinct advantage over the nonmembers. Not only that, the committee is usually united behind the recommendation and already has several votes in favor of their position. Most boards are congenial and do not wish to embarrass fellow trustees by rejecting their recommendations, though it does happen occasionally. Most often when this happens, the matter is referred back to the committee for further study. When this occurs, the committee will call for further research and may modify its position or may not.

TIPS FOR GETTING ALONG WITH COMMITTEES

Information prepared for the committee must be given to all members of the committee at the same time. There is always a temptation for the library director to seek out the chair or certain other members of the committee who appear to be more interested in the matter at hand than others, and give them advance information before it is made available to others. This should always be avoided. All members of the committee need to be on the same footing. Time and date of meeting need to be set when all members of the committee can come, not just a majority. As the committee increases in size, this goal becomes more difficult, but it needs to be addressed just the same. No one likes to be left out of an important meeting. The library trustee who is left out may become an adversary instead of a supporter.

Committee meetings run smoothly if a little advance planning is done. Never meet without an agenda provided to members prior to the appointed time. Always include the charge made to the committee by the board (why are we meeting?). Leave space on the agenda so that other areas within the jurisdiction of the committee may be discussed if time permits. Sending out the agenda beforehand will often interest a trustee in attending a meeting instead of skipping it. Always do a practice run-through of the agenda on your own before the meeting to make sure everything goes according to plan and that you have all of the information needed. Play the devil's advocate and anticipate some of the questions you may have to answer when the committee meets. "The effective man always states at the outset of a meeting the specific purpose and contribution it is to achieve. He always, at the end of his meetings, goes back to the opening statement and relates the final conclusions to the original intent."[10]

Try to limit the duration of the meeting to no more than one hour whenever possible. If the discussion extends beyond that limit, another meeting should be scheduled. One of the advantages in meeting over lunch is that the discussion rarely extends past the one-hour time frame due to other obligations for committee members. If meetings in public places are too distracting for your trustees, by all means schedule them in a quiet meeting room.

Make sure that everyone has the opportunity to voice his or her opinion. Even though the group is small, there is no absolute guarantee that every person will be heard. If someone is not contributing, the chair should solicit an opinion. Sometimes one person will try to dominate the discussion by talking nonstop, but when this happens, the committee chair can tactfully ask others for their viewpoints. The library director's input should be consciously limited and never dominate the discussion. If the discussion starts to ramble and move away from the problem, the library director can bring it back into focus with a question or two.

Sometimes, complete agreement cannot be reached in committee. In that case, the minority opinion still has a right to be heard. Suppose, for example, that one of the members of the Anytown Public Library Board's Operations Committee felt that the students' demands should be followed to the letter—amending the budget so that the library could be open from 9:00 a.m. to 10:00 p.m. If that trustee is determined and refuses to bow to the majority will of the committee, it is better to note his or her opposition in the recommendation to the board than to ignore it. Only rarely will a minority view make it through the committee meeting, but it does happen once in awhile. By putting the minority view in the report, you are able to recognize the divergent opinion and give that member the opportunity to present an opposing argument to the board. A member with a dissenting opinion is less likely to stir up trouble at the board meeting if he or she knows that that opinion will be acknowledged and addressed.

It is very important to write up the minutes of the meeting as soon as possible and to mail a copy to each member of the committee. This will solidify the ideas discussed and help provide unanimity when the committee presents its recommendations to the board. It will also give committee members the opportunity to clarify positions and correct errors in the perceived actions taken in committee. In these minutes, it is better to use broad enveloping terms like "consensus of members," "the committee believes," and "members felt that," rather than attributing ideas to specific members of the committee.

SUMMARY

The committee structure of the library board works most effectively when the number of members is small. Standing and special committees function best when they have been given a specific task by the parent library board. The committee structure is effective in integrating new trustees into the operation of the library board. Committee meetings are useful when they respond to a problem with a constructive recommendation to the board. The library director must work with the committees if the library is to be improved.

ENDNOTES

1. John K. Brilhart, *Effective Group Discussion*. 5th ed. Dubuque, IA: William C. Brown, 1986. p. 58.

2. Diane J. Duca, *Nonprofit Boards: A Practical Guide to Roles, Responsibilities, and Performance*. Phoenix, AZ: The Oryx Press, 1986. p. 24.

3. Michael C. Thomsett, *The Little Black Book of Business Meetings*. New York: American Management Association, 1989. p. 11.

4. Duca, pp. 24-25.

5. Brilhart, p. 79.

6. Duca, p. x.

7. It always surprises me when trustees currently serving on my library board have little or no idea of the hours the library is open. It is a good idea, therefore, when a committee or library director makes a recommendation concerning an hours change for the library, to restate the current hours of opening.

8. It is important to convey to the board that the committee did meet and a quorum was present to legitimize the committee's recommendation. If the committee met more than once or held public hearings on the matter, that also needs to be related to the board. Committee members who attended the meeting may be listed by name in the recommendation.

9. Ellen Altman, ed. *Local Public Library Administration*. 2nd ed. Chicago: American Library Association, 1980. p. 101.

10. Peter F. Drucker, *The Effective Executive*. New York: Harper and Row, 1967. p. 69.

BOARD MEETINGS

Working effectively with library trustees at the board meeting is what making progress for the library is all about. It is at the regularly scheduled meetings of the board that the decisions will be made which will eventually determine the adequacy of the library, its collections, personnel, and programs. Learning to work *with* your board is vital to library improvement.

FREQUENCY AND TIME OF MEETING

The bylaws of the library board will determine how often the trustees will meet and the time of the meeting. How often should the board meet? My feeling is that many library boards meet too often rather than not often enough. I prefer regularly scheduled meetings on a quarterly basis with special meetings called when the need arises, but guidelines and standards often call for library boards to meet more frequently.[1] Many boards meet on a monthly basis. In fact my survey of library directors indicated that monthly meetings are by far the most common frequency for public libraries in the United States and Canada. Seventy-three percent of the library directors who responded to the question served library boards that met monthly. The next most popular frequency of board meetings was quarterly, but only 8 1/2 percent of the library boards had only four regular meetings per year.

When the board meets too often, there is a tendency for the administrator to have to "create" business for the board rather than to deal with real policy issues. Trustees are not stupid—they know when they are being asked to discuss trivialities and handle "busy-work." It seems to me that it is better for the library program in the long run for the board to meet on a regular basis, with an interval between meetings that allows for meaningful policy questions to develop. Also, when the board is asked to deal with less meaningful items of business, it has the tendency to wander over from policy making into library administration, which creates its own set of problems and difficulties. The survey showed that most library directors were satisfied with the number of meetings their library boards had per year. Better than 90 percent felt that the frequency of their board's meetings was "just right." Of the remaining 10 percent, half felt their boards met too often and the other half felt they did not meet often enough.

Frequent meetings can become meaningless and the trustee, realizing that the decisions being made will have little or no effect on improving the library, will begin to stay away from these meetings. Library board meetings should have on their agenda a number of items which will materially affect the library, its operation, and its adequacy. Business of this nature is not all that prevalent, especially after the library director has been at his position for several years, and can best be handled at one meeting rather than spread out over three. "Lower rates of participation are closely associated with lower satisfaction with a group."[2]

The time and place of the meeting should be decided by the board at its organizational meeting (usually the first regular meeting of each year). One of the advantages of meeting at the library is that the administrator can actually show trustees areas of the building which would be affected by architectural changes, new furniture, shelving, policy changes, etc. It should not be a hard and fast rule that the board *must* meet at the library, however. It is more important that the trustees meet in pleasant, quiet surroundings, away from distracting influences. Privacy is another factor which is conducive to effective group meetings.[3]

The Anytown Public Library Board met in the library's meeting room for many years, but a time came when the room needed to be converted to other purposes and a new location for the meetings had to be found. There are certain factors involved in choosing a site for board meetings. It should be within walking distance of the library if not in the library itself. At the same time, it should be easily accessible to the public, should observers wish to attend meetings. As its new meeting location, the Anytown Library Board chose a vacant room in city hall, which was in the same block as the library. It had the advantage of having an outside entrance which was always open during the board meetings.

Actual time of meeting, again, is decided by the trustees. Of course, library boards meet at all sorts of different times. Some have morning meetings, while others meet in the afternoon or evening. It will depend upon when the members are available, and the time may change as the make-up of the board changes. The Carroll Public Library Board met for many years at eight o'clock in the evening. Then a surgeon was appointed to the board who had to rise early in the morning and the board changed its meeting time to 7:00 p.m. to accommodate his schedule. Still later, members decided that they didn't want to go out at night, particularly during the winter months, so they changed the time of their meeting to 5:15 p.m.

REFRESHMENTS

We have found that serving food at meetings of the library board is beneficial. Actually, I discovered this option once when I was interviewing at another, larger library. At the interview, which was conducted by the full board, coffee and donuts were served. It seemed like a great idea, so when I returned to my library, we provided homemade cookies and coffee at the next board meeting. It was an instant success and the practice has continued with only the food changing. At a summer meeting we may serve fresh fruit, and during the winter months, cheese and crackers and various other snack items are popular. Stay away from food requiring spoons or forks—finger food is best. I usually have several plates of snacks on the table within reach of everyone, and the coffee is on a table near the entrance of the room so that trustees may fill a cup on their way into the meeting.

Coffee is always served, and sometimes I provide an alternative beverage like lemonade or cider. The trustees have been very appreciative and it has promoted a more friendly atmosphere at board meetings. I feel that library trustees do not reap any great rewards for serving on the library board. They seem to be a somewhat hidden board most of the time—that is, until there is major discord at the library and then they receive a lot of unwanted attention. Providing food at a board meeting is a small perk for otherwise often unappreciated work! At one time, the majority on my board smoked cigarettes during the meeting, and several of us went home with sinus congestion and headaches from the second-hand smoke. Then at one meeting, I forgot to place ashtrays on the table. To my astonishment no one smoked! Since then, I never put out ashtrays and no one has smoked or complained about not being able to smoke.

THE TABLE

"Settings for board meetings should aim for comfort, efficiency and adequate seating; constancy of location, (i.e., not being shuttled from one room to another each time the board meets) adequate lighting and ventilation; provision of simple refreshments; a clean table on which to work. . ."[4] If you feel that constructive group decisions are not being made at your board meetings and that everyone is not participating, you may wish to examine your table and your seating arrangements. Studies have shown that a circular table with group members seated closely together leads to more productive group discussion.[5] "At a rectangular table, such as is frequently found in a meeting room, persons at the corners contribute least to the discussion, whereas members of the group at the ends and central position on the sides speak more often."[6] While this may be true in some group situations, I've found that the outspoken person who wishes to be heard on every issue (and every library board seems to have one of these individuals) will dominate the discussion no matter where he or she sits!

ORDER OF BUSINESS

To remove all doubt and provide for consistency from meeting to meeting, the exact order of business at regular meetings of the library board should be stated in the board's bylaws. At meetings of the Anytown Public Library's board of trustees, for example, the order of business is as follows:

- Call to order by the president of the board
- Reading and approval of the minutes of the previous meeting
- Reading and approval of the bills
- Correspondence
- Report of the library director
- Committee reports
- Unfinished business
- New business
- Setting the time for the next meeting
- Adjournment

The order of business will vary from board to board. Some library boards have, as one item in the order of business, the approval of the agenda. Others would not have the item to set the time for the next meeting for it would already have been set in the bylaws. The order of business shown above is merely one example—it works for the library board in Anytown and it may or may not work at your library. The exact order of business and the items in the order will be determined by each individual library board and written into their bylaws. It is important, once the order of business has been established in the bylaws, for the group to stick to it.

USE DESCRIPTIVE LANGUAGE
On the agenda, under each category, the items of business are listed. Be as descriptive as you can be in one sentence. Instead of listing an item as "hours change" it is better to state "proposal to

eliminate Friday evening library hours." This will give trustees more of an idea of the items to be discussed and perhaps make them more interested in attending the meeting. If low attendance at board meetings is a problem, it may be because the agenda is perceived as being boring. Spice it up with more provacative wording and you may be able to entice your trustees to the meetings.

Another point to remember when preparing the agenda is to leave an open item under the categories of correspondence, unfinished, and new business. This provides trustees with an opportunity to discuss items not placed on the agenda beforehand. Perhaps a trustee has received a letter or telephone call just before the meeting about something which needs to be discussed by the board as soon as possible. My experience in this regard is that "other business" is rarely brought up for discussion under the "other" category, but it is still wise to provide an opportunity for free expression of other ideas should trustees wish to discuss them. In this way, the trustees do not feel stifled. They know that they will be able to bring up problems during the meeting without formally asking that they be included on the agenda. This practice may lead to surprises for the library director, but the right of free expression by trustees outweighs this potential problem.

GROUP RELATED ITEMS

Related items of business should be grouped together whenever possible. If you plan to discuss wage scales for library employees in general and also have a proposal to raise pages to the minimum wage—these items should be placed together on the agenda if at all possible. They might even be combined into a broader single item of business. Sometimes it will not be possible to place them in close proximity on the agenda, as in instances where one item is found under old business and another under new business. Often though, in such a circumstance, the library director can ask the trustees to defer discussion on one item and consider both matters together.

The late Fred Wezeman, professor in the public library field at the University of Minnesota and later director of the School of Library and Information Sciences at the University of Iowa, suggested to his students that at least two items be placed on every library board meeting agenda which the library board could reject without seriously damaging the library program. My experience with this strategy has been very positive. Trustees do not wish to rubber stamp the ideas of library directors, no matter how wonderful these ideas may be. To do so consistently would seriously undermine their power and make their positions meaningless. The idea is to have items on the agenda which the board can vote against, so that they will see themselves functioning in an acceptable way. I cannot remember a board meeting where every item was approved and it is better to have nonconsequential items rejected than to have the same fate befall important items. So, I always have a couple items of business on every agenda which, if rejected by the board, will not have any major impact or detrimental effect on the library. There is a danger in this procedure, however, and that is that occasionally the item will *not* be rejected but will be adopted by the board and become a part of library or board policy.

One must be careful to choose items that, if adopted, won't hurt the program. A proposal to purchase an expensive item of equipment like a microfilm/fiche reader-printer is a good example. Funding is probably not available within the budget to allow for this unplanned capital expenditure. The board rejects the item and may suggest that it be included in the next budget proposal. If the board *did* find the money to purchase the item, it would be a positive step for the library, but if it didn't, it wouldn't harm the program. I suggested to my board that a blinking neon "open tonight" sign be purchased and mounted on the outside of the building. They rejected the idea as "too flashy." Had they adopted it, however, it would not have had negative effects.

Deciding which items to include on the agenda may fall to the library director, the president of the library board, or a combination of both, and may vary at the same library from time to time. I generally make the decisions about agenda items on my own but library trustees can, at any time, request that an item be discussed at the meeting. In years past, some of our board presidents have visited with me before the agenda was proposed and suggested that certain items be added. Business for each meeting comes up during the days following the previous meeting and items can be written down as they occur for use when building the agenda for the next meeting.

A tentative agenda should be mailed out to all trustees a few days before the meeting. Tentative means that by the time of the meeting, the agenda may have been changed, with new items added and/or old items dropped depending upon the circumstances. Figure 5-1 is an example of the tentative agenda sent out to library trustees of the Anytown Public Library for the fall quarterly meeting.

After receiving their tentative agendas in the mail, trustees may call with additional items they wish to have discussed at the meeting. Often, the items they call in are actually already included

FIGURE 5-1   Tentative Board Meeting Agenda

Anytown Public Library Board Meeting
September 15, 1991

TENTATIVE AGENDA

CALL TO ORDER -- President James Smith

READING OF THE MINUTES of June 14, 1991 regular meeting

READING OF THE BILLS: June 14, 1991 -- Septmeber 15, 1991

CORRESPONDENCE

1. Letter from Annabel Foster concerning donation of her doll collection to the Anytown Public Library

2. Other?

REPORT OF THE LIBRARY DIRECTOR: September 15, 1991

COMMITTEE REPORTS

1. Ways and Means Committee -- Dr. Peterson

UNFINISHED BUSINESS

1. Results of study into the question of adding a second telephone line

2. Discussion of the lack of parking spaces for library patrons

3. Appointment of Library Board standing committees -- President James Smith

4. Final report on the summer reading program for children

5. Other?

NEW BUSINESS

1. Proposal to raise the fee charged to nonresidents to use the Anytown Public Library

2. Recommendation to raise library pages to the new minimum wage

3. Proposal to grant reciprocal borrowing privileges to patrons of other libraries in the county

4. Discussion of the possible use of volunteers in the library

5. Other?

SETTING THE DATE & TIME FOR THE NEXT MEETING

ADJOURNMENT

but because each item is limited to one descriptive sentence, it is not obvious. In this case, the trustee needs to be told where the item of interest will appear. For example, after receiving the agenda for one of our regular quarterly library board meetings, a trustee called and wanted to know why there was no report listed from a special committee which was seeking a grant for the library. That item could have been included under committee reports but, in this instance, the matter was covered in the library director's report. This trustee needed to know that. If the item is not on the agenda, it can be added.

Trustees should have the right to place on the agenda items they feel are important for the library board to discuss, and the director should make certain that this right is honored. Some items may be dropped if anticipated attendance at the meeting is low. I once sent out a tentative agenda to the board with an item calling for a discussion of theft and mutilation of library materials. This would be a very important issue and required every trustee's input. On the day of the meeting we were having difficulty even finding a quorum so the item was dropped from the final agenda. It was discussed at a later meeting.

After the agenda has been finalized and copied for the meeting, it should also be posted in the library. In this way, public notice of the meeting is given to those who are most interested in the library and its future: the staff and the library's users. Notice of the meeting, with or without the agenda (depending upon local custom and practice), should also be sent to the media. If the agenda is sent to the media, it must be the final agenda, not the tentative one. My feeling is that the agenda need not be sent to the media, but that the notification of the meeting state that the agenda will be posted at the library. On the day of the board meeting, a staff member reminds each trustee of the meeting by phone and determines probable attendance. In this way we will know if we will have a quorum well in advance of the meeting time, and can cancel if we know a quorum will not be present.

PREPARING FOR THE MEETING

The officers of the board, particularly the president, may wish to meet with the library director prior to the meeting. About half of the board presidents I have served with have indicated that they wanted to meet with me before the meeting either to work on the agenda or more often to find out my thoughts on the items already on the agenda. In my experience, it hasn't seemed to matter much whether I went over the agenda with the president before the meeting or not. Some presidents wish to appear more knowledgeable than other trustees at the meeting, while others seem prepared to go into the meeting on the same footing as the rest of the board members.

GET IT IN WRITING

For me, preparations for the meeting center around the computer and the copy machine! I prefer to have a written report, recommendation, or communication of some sort for nearly every item on the agenda. I do this for several reasons. First, I think more clearly if each item of business is written down and in front of me. Second, I think trustees are happier if they have a written recommendation in hand—not only will it be better understood at the meeting, but it will also give them a piece of paper to take home with them. They may keep it for future reference or they may read it over and get rid of it, but it is important for them to know exactly what my recommendation was on every matter, even though that recommendation may not have been adopted. Finally, a written report or recommendation will be useful to me in preparing for future discussions or reports and in preparing news releases for the media. Too often, with oral discussions, suggestions, and recommendations, one leaves with only a vague idea of what actually happened and what the library director recommended. I want my board to know where I stand on each issue and exactly what I am proposing for the library. A written proposal makes this possible.

There are some matters which will not require a written communication. A few items are so brief and easily solved that a background paper is not justified. It is up to the library director to decide how much preparation is needed for each item on the agenda and how best to present the necessary information which will lead to a decision by the board.

USE YOUR COMPUTER

Several days before the actual meeting, I begin to do paperwork in preparation for the meeting. A personal computer is a necessity in this process for it allows one to put thoughts down and easily go back and change them many times before arriving at the final, polished paper. I use a single floppy disk for library board meetings. It has the form for the library director's report so that I will only need to change the data regarding receipts, disbursements, and statistics and compose the written part. This saves a considerable amount of preparation time and also serves to standardize the report from one meeting to the next. Saving the report presented at the previous meeting makes it very easy to do the new report, and is also a great help at the end of the year, in preparing the annual report. I also keep a paper copy of previous director's reports in a looseleaf notebook to help me in the written "state of the library" part of each new director's report.

Copies of all papers for the board are made on the copy machine using various colors of paper, so that at the meeting the trustees can be referred to a report by color. I can say, for example, "the proposal to eliminate Friday evening hours at the library is the one on green paper." Even though the papers are in order at each trustee's place at the table when the meeting begins, often by the time the business is taken up, they are no longer in order because the trustee has moved ahead picking out proposals which are of particular interest and put them back out of order.

Sometimes, trustees will ask that paperwork be mailed to them ahead of time so that they can study it and not have to make a decision without really having had time to look into the matter. This is a concept that is frequently mentioned in books and articles and it is worth experimenting with.[7] However, I have tried this procedure on occasion, and I don't feel that it works very well for everything because some library trustees won't read the material no matter how far ahead they receive it. What happens then is that some trustees have delved deeply into the problem while others have no knowledge of it at all, and that tends to put those who have not done their homework at a distinct disadvantage. Too often, then, the decision is made by a handful of people and the others feel left out.

One might argue that continuing to follow this practice would eventually result in everyone reading the material before the meeting, but it doesn't seem to work that way. Quite often, the very person who demanded that the material be sent out ahead of time is the one who didn't find time to read it. I feel that it is better to have every trustee on the same level of knowledge at the meeting if possible. The library director can then read through the report and recommendations, there will be ample time to discuss it, and a decision will be reached without prior study. There is another danger in sending out your recommendations ahead of time. There always seem to be one or two trustees on the board who are negative and not really interested in improving the library. By sending out information to these people before the meeting, you are inviting them to prepare opposition to the proposal and to come up with arguments (either individually or collectively) against your position.

THE RUN-THROUGH

Perhaps the most useful way to prepare for a library board meeting is for the library director to sit down and do an actual run-through of the agenda. More often than not the director will discover that a report or recommendation is weak and needs strengthening or that the paperwork for an item on the agenda is lacking. For items of business where a paper has not been prepared, I will run through the material in my mind and jot down thoughts on a scratch pad or make brief notes on my copy of the agenda so that when the item comes up for discussion, I won't be faced with a blank mind or forget important points. The run-through will also allow the director to play "the devil's advocate" and anticipate potential arguments and questions. I take a copy of the agenda and copies of the report, recommendation, or background information for each item on the agenda with me and sit, by myself, at a table (not necessarily at the site of the meeting) several hours before meeting time. There I mentally go through the meeting step-by-step. If needed, I will have the time to revise reports, arguments, and recommendations before the meeting. Even if I don't discover changes which need to be made, the mental run-through of the meeting will prepare me for almost everything which will occur at the actual meeting.

EDUCATING THE BOARD

One of the difficulties with the concept of library board decisions is that a professionally trained library director must rely on relatively unprepared or unaware trustees to establish policies which will move the library to a high level of adequacy. Trustees may be well-educated in their own fields and yet be largely ignorant regarding what constitutes good library service. It is only natural for trustees to attempt to apply knowledge from other fields to the library, with mixed results. Sometimes there can be a transfer of knowledge and experience from business to the public library, but there are often aspects which are peculiar just to libraries.

It is, therefore, very important for the library director to *educate* the trustees about the library. This is a fact recognized by most practicing public library directors. In my survey I asked librarians to give advice to a recent library school graduate about working with a library board. The response given most frequently was to educate and inform library trustees. A librarian from Maine wrote: "Be proactive in educating these nonlibrarians about library specific things (they may know about budgets or building maintenance but nothing about MARC or intellectual freedom)."

This is an ongoing process and one in which the same information must be repeated over and over again until it becomes integrated into the thinking of the trustees. Because library policy is not the primary concern in the lives of most trustees, it takes repeated exposure to bring the average trustee to the level of awareness needed to act responsibly in the library's behalf. I am sure most library directors can remember a critical time—perhaps the defense of the budget to the funding authorities—when one of our trustees rose and presented a string of totally false information about the library. At times like these there seems to be no place to hide!

Educating the library trustee is a full-time job. It happens at meetings, it happens between meetings, but it must be a continual effort on the part of the library director. For this reason, it is very important to keep all trustees informed at all times. Of particular importance is the matter of keeping the trustee who does not attend every meeting informed. Merely sending a copy of the minutes of the missed meeting is not enough. The absent trustee needs to receive everything prepared for those who attended the meeting— the reports, the recommendations, the background material—all of it. Occasionally, a trustee who has missed a meeting will come to the library director or other trustee and ask to be updated on the meeting, but in my experience this occurs only rarely. It is very important, then, for the sake of his or her education and continuity, to be given the opportunity to understand the action which took place, and this can be done by sending the necessary information after the meeting and even visiting with that trustee in person or on the telephone at the director's initiative.

GIVE REPORTS TO TRUSTEES

One of the best ways to educate trustees is by report. At each meeting, I present a number of reports on various aspects of library operation. These are not always proposals for action or policy changes but merely progress reports to educate trustees on a variety of library-related topics. For example, each fall I present a report on the summer reading program. In this report I discuss the program in detail, showing how the program operated, what we hoped it would achieve, how it worked, which staff members were involved, how many children joined, what the requirements were, how many earned certificates, what incentives were given, what it cost, etc. I compare this year's program with those in previous years and indicate what changes might be made next year. After reading this report to the board, I ask them for comments and take notes on their ideas for possible inclusion in next summer's reading program. If a trustee makes a plausible suggestion, I will try to work it into next summer's program if at all possible, and that change will become a part of next fall's report. It is very important to be open to trustee input. A library director from the West coast wrote: "Be open to suggestions and discussion presented by members of the board. In many instances their views on community needs provide a necessary perspective of a community when devloping goals, objectives, and services." This process of reporting is edifying for the board and, even though some of the information will be forgotten by this time next year, much is retained by trustees and used in later decisions concerning the children's program of our library.

VISIT OTHER LIBRARIES

Another good way to educate trustees is by taking them to library meetings and encouraging them to go to meetings with other trustees. One of the problems with meetings, however, is that they vary so widely in content, presentation, and applicability. Some meetings are poorly planned and executed, and a trustee would gain a poor impression of library professionals. Still, meetings widen trustee horizons and encourage thinking about the library in new and different ways, and for this reason may be very profitable. It can be difficult for library trustees to find the time to go to library meetings, but it is often worth the effort. I once persuaded the staff of the regional library system to present a trustee workshop at my library (which is in a remote corner of the region) and only one of my trustees found the time to attend!

Library trustees may receive firsthand education if you suggest that when they visit other communities on business or vacation they make it a point to tour the local public library. Although there are great similarities among public libraries, there are also very noticeable differences. Observing how different libraries handle problems similar to those we encounter is often a good education for the library trustee. As likely as not, he or she will come back to our meetings with a better appreciation of our own library, but may also bring new ideas on policies and operations which are worth applying in the local situation. Be receptive to new ideas from trustees. Encourage them to seek out new solutions to old problems.

ENCOURAGING PARTICIPATION

Studies have shown that "as the size of a group increases, the opportunity for each member to participate in discussion decreases."[8] The larger the board, the easier it is for some trustees *not* to express an opinion—even if the matter is of vital concern to the individual. A library director from Minnesota who worked for a board with 25 members wrote: "Work with a board of five to seven trustees. Mine is too big to keep tabs on what everyone is thinking."

GET EVERY TRUSTEE INVOLVED

One must remember that shyness is not a barrier to being appointed to a library board. People who are uncomfortable expressing themselves in public are appointed to library boards just as outspoken individuals are appointed. On my library board, they have been a small minority, but they present a unique challenge. Their opinions are important and the board president and library director need to find creative ways to get them to participate in the discussions on library matters.

Each library trustee has a unique point of view and brings to each meeting a large and varied set of experiences which can have an impact on any decisions made by the board. It is well to remember that solutions to library problems can come from anyone in the group and often one unreasonable idea will stimulate the thinking of another person and lead to a workable solution.[9] "Group judgments are generally superior to those of one individual because the judgments are evaluated and refined by several people with varying skills and perspectives."[10] But in order for the library board to function properly and to make wise decisions for the library, every trustee's viewpoint must be heard.

One technique is to go around the table and ask for comments member by member, or to call on one or two trustees and ask them to speak about the issue at hand. This is a distinctly uncomfortable situation and even then some people may defer comment by saying "I feel the same way as Mrs. King about this," and not elaborate. It isn't good for any board to have as a member someone who is unable or unwilling to express an opinion. Every trustee has a vote and it is important to discover how each trustee feels about the matter under consideration before calling for the vote. The trustee who does not express an opinion may prove to have the deciding vote on a critical issue. A skillful president will try in many ways to elicit participation from members who are not contributing to the discussion.

DISCOURAGE FILIBUSTERS

The opposite situation is much more prevalent, in which one or two trustees seek to dominate and control the discussion. Here again, a skillful president will seek to limit the contributions of the more outspoken, but it can be difficult. Calling on individuals who have not stated an opinion is one option. The library director can also intervene by asking for the ideas of others, but must do so carefully, so as not to appear to be usurping the duties of an inept board president. It becomes an even more difficult situation when one does not have "a skillful board president," which is often the case. Sometimes it is the board president who is the problem. This is usually not as difficult a situation on an advisory board as it would be on a governing board. A Utah library director comments: "Evaluate each board member/situation as boards are not always alike. Advisory boards are usually easier to work with. Authority boards can become difficult if you have a dictator type member or chairman who may want to control."

Leadership is critical for the library board to operate effectively. Fortunately, leadership is not limited to the stated board officers. "Every group has at least one leader. The leader may be the formal, designated leader or an informal leader who holds no specific title but is able to influence group behavior and help the group work towards its goal."[11]

Another problem which inhibits free discussion and participation by all members of the board is caused by the library director who takes the floor for a disproportionate amount of time. As library director, you need constantly to remind yourself not to talk too much during a board meeting. Holding one's tongue is often difficult because, presumably, the library director has a lot at stake. When the decision has been made and the dust has settled, the library trustees leave and go home; it is the library director who is stuck with attempting to apply a possibly unworkable policy. Still, the library director can express his or her opinion on an issue succinctly during the time of discussion, without monopolizing the allotted time.

Library board meetings are only worthwhile when they accomplish something— when the group can achieve positive results and solutions.[12] Full participation by all members of the library board is necessary to achieve this goal. Every member of the board shares the responsibility for effective decision making.[13] The decision making process is not necessarily an easy one but works best when a wide diversity of views is presented. This is why full participation is essential. "A decision is a judgment. It is a choice between alternatives. It is rarely a choice between right and wrong. It is at best a choice between 'almost right' and 'probably wrong'—but much more often a choice between two courses of action, neither of which is probably more nearly right than the other."[14]

PREVENTING NEGATIVE ACTION BY THE BOARD

There will be times at library board meetings when trustees vote down proposals which the library director feels are very important to the library and its future.[15] Sometimes nothing can be done to prevent such action, while at other times tactics can be used which, though not always resulting in positive action, can delay or defer the negative. One such tactic is to refer the problem to committee for further study. It is often easier to research a matter in a small group and persuade that group to help reverse the thinking expressed at the board meeting.

At the Anytown Public Library, for example, the director proposed that the Library close at 6:00 p.m. on Friday evenings since use of the library had declined drastically due to school events on that night. The recent decision to open downtown stores on Thursday nights instead of Friday nights also contributed to lower library use by eliminating people who came downtown to shop and also to use the library. The director did not see this problem as one which would be vigorously opposed by anyone on the library board and so had prepared a brief written recommendation based on cost and lack of use data. At the board meeting, however, three trustees were very vocal in their opposition to the matter and the rest seemed indifferent at best. Trustees who are indifferent or have no strong position tend to go along with those who speak out because they don't wish to offend anyone and don't view the situation as a critical area for the library.

REFERRING ITEMS TO COMMITTEE

The library director at Anytown, sensing that the proposal would be defeated if it came to a vote, suggested that it be referred to the operations committee for further study and recommendations at the next meeting. Once the library board votes in favor or against an item it becomes very difficult to reverse the decision. Referring it to committee, however, keeps the issue alive and holds out the potential for reversing the viewpoints of those trustees set on opposing a proposal. This committee at Anytown was composed of one of the trustees who vocally opposed Friday night closings and also contained two trustees who were indifferent to the matter. The committee meeting forced one trustee to reassess his position and caused two more to take a position.

Referring an item to committee for further study is not a guarantee that negative action will not occur, but it does give the proposal a second opportunity. In the example of the Anytown Public Library closing on Friday evenings, the committee studied the problem in detail and, for various reasons, recommended that the Library remain open during those hours. The library board voted to go along with the committee, and once that decision was made, there would have to be significant changes in the situation before it could be brought to the board's attention again. The library director at Anytown must have new data in order to reopen the subject. Library trustees do not appreciate making a decision only to have it brought up for discussion again at a later date when the circumstances have not changed.

VOTING TO "TABLE" ITEMS

Another way to prevent or delay action is to table the matter. This ploy is of particular use when tempers flare and a heated argument occurs. Voting to table the matter means that it may be discussed at a future meeting when, perhaps, feelings are not running quite so high. Again, there is no guarantee that negative action will be prevented—it may prove to be only delaying the inevitable, but it is a tactic which is sometimes deployed at a board meeting. The library director will have to be careful in suggesting that the item be tabled, it will be much better if the suggestion comes from a trustee or the board president. Once tabled, it will usually, but not always, be at the library director's discretion to decide when the problem is to be examined once more. He may wish to wait until conditions are more favorable to add it to the board's agenda. When a situation like this occurs it is very tempting to delay bringing up a previously tabled problem until a meeting when the director knows that the most vocal opponent will be absent. Opposition has its own value in the decision-making process and should not be pushed aside carelessly.

VOTING PROCEDURES

Voting patterns on library boards are intriguing. Generally our board passes motions on a voice vote. There are problems with that because a voice vote does not always reflect everyone's opinions and feelings about the matter at hand. Only rarely has anyone voted against a motion at one of this board's meetings. It takes real courage for a trustee to vote no when he thinks everyone else is voting yes. One way to get around this problem is to ask for individual votes or a secret ballot, but even then few trustees will dare oppose the majority view, and most will know the majority view by following the discussion before the vote. There are library boards, of course, where there has been a history of open disagreement, and split votes will be the rule rather than the exception.

The way trustees vote is interesting when there *is* a division of opinion. At one of the meetings of the library board early in my tenure as library director, the topic of concern was whether the board should authorize the purchase of window air conditioners or have the small Carnegie building centrally air conditioned. The discussion was heated and it was obvious that opinion was fairly evenly divided. As a young librarian fresh out of library school, I sat somewhat open mouthed as the arguments swirled around me. They never asked for my opinion, and had they done so I would have told them that I would be happy with either option after surviving a long, hot Iowa summer with only a small electric fan in my office!

Eventually the board president called for the vote and did so by going around the table and asking each individual. The motion was for central air conditioning, and as the vote was taken the Catholic members all voted against the motion and the Protestant members all voted for it. As fate would have it the Protestants held the majority by one seat on the board and the library was soon centrally air conditioned! The Catholics had argued that if the library added window air conditioners and then moved to another location, the air conditioning units could be moved as well. I always wondered if there was some religious significance involved in one type of air conditioning as opposed to the other, but never came to any conclusion. Ten years later the library moved to a new building which didn't have *any* windows so, perhaps the Protestants on my board were gifted with second sight!

Delicate matters do come up before the library board from time to time and can be handled best with a secret ballot. I can only remember one time in the association with my library board when a secret ballot was taken, however. It was a difficult situation where a clerical member of the staff had written a poison-pen letter to the library director and the board was deciding whether or not the individual should be fired. It was felt that a secret ballot would preserve anonymity for trustees, but as it happened, the vote was unanimous in favor of the firing. Secret ballots can be useful because trustees who feel strongly about an item can vote the way they really believe they should rather than to go along with the others just to keep the peace. Again, the call for a secret ballot should come from a trustee, not the library director.

FOLLOWING UP

Making the decision is important, but it is also necessary to implement the decision and follow up on it. "It is not enough for everyone to agree on what should be done. Someone must assume specific responsibility for follow-up."[16] That "someone" is going to be you, for it is your job as library director to implement the policies the board decides upon. Again, it is important to separate the role of the board from that of the director. As a Tennessee library director recommends: "Strive to maintain a good working relationship with all members of the board. Keep them informed on what is happening at your library. Let them know that you value their cooperation, but remember that you must make all the day-to-day decisions about what is done in the library. Their job is to make the policies; your job is to carry the policies out as you operate the library."

After the library board meeting has adjourned, the decisions made by the board must be followed up. When a policy is adopted or altered by the trustees, the library director needs to keep them informed as to the results of their action. This can be covered at the next meeting in the library director's report, or the data can be effectively presented in a special follow-up report. It is important to keep statistics on the change and to present them in a factual way—leaving out the library director's own value judgements. One of the few compliments I ever received from one particular trustee was because of my follow-up report on a matter he and I had disagreed upon at a board meeting.[17] The board had voted to open the library on Sunday afternoons, something I felt was not necessary in our community. My follow-up report at the next meeting showed that while circulation on Sundays had not been the unmitigated success the board had hoped for, there *were* significant numbers of people coming to the library on Sunday afternoons. The trustee who had pushed for the new hours had trouble believing that I would present the facts without trying to skew them to reflect my personal feelings. Be honest with your library board at all times. If you alter the facts or present a biased report even once, you will lose credibility with your board, and credibility is what is most needed to improve the library in your community. In fact, honesty showed up in my survey as one of the necessary ingredients when dealing with library trustees. It was mentioned frequently as being an important part of a working philosophy in library director/library board relationships. Follow the advice of a Maryland library director: "Be honest with your board. Tell them more than they want to know rather than less than they need."

SIMPLIFY TAKING THE MINUTES
Taking the minutes of the board meeting is one of those tedious jobs which needs to be passed around among the library trustees. We have found that a simple form sheet such as the one shown in Figure 5-2 greatly simplifies the drudgery. The names of the trustees are entered near the top of the sheet, and the person taking the minutes at the meetings only needs to circle the names of those who are present. A series of blank spaces under different categories of library board business allow for motions to be written in.

The minutes of each meeting should be entered into the permanent minutes book and copies made and sent to library trustees as soon as possible. This action will immediately refresh their memories of the meeting and will probably eliminate corrections of the minutes at the next meeting when the distant past is no longer remembered accurately. Try not to use specific trustees' names in the minutes other than for motions made and seconded (even there, just the fact that a motion was made and seconded may be enough). The decision to use names of trustees making and seconding motions will depend, of course, on the custom of your board. It is useful to place in the minutes the gist of the discussion, particularly if no action is taken; but it is better to use phrases like "the consensus of the trustees was," "some trustees felt," "the majority seemed to believe," etc. rather than saying "Dr. Peterson said. . ." Direct quotes have a way of coming back to haunt you and the trustee in question will tell you at the next meeting that he never said that and ask for it to be struck from the minutes. Try to make the minutes as interesting as possible while conveying the actions the board takes. There is nothing quite so boring as strictly relating motions and their passage without providing some of the background detail and discussion which led to the final vote. The

FIGURE 5-2

Library Board Minutes

Date:_____

Trustees present:_____

_____

Others attending:_____

_____

Meeting called to order by:_____

Minutes read for:_____

    additions or corrections:_____

_____

    approval moved by:_____
    seconded by_____
    carried? Y N

Bills read for:_____

    additions or corrections:_____

_____

    approval moved by:_____
    seconded by:_____
    carried? Y N

Continued

FIGURE 5-2 *Continued*

Correspondence:

action taken:_____
_____
_____
_____

Library Director's report:

comments made:_____
_____

approval moved by:_____
seconded by:_____
carried? Y N

Old business:

motion made_____
_____

approval moved by:_____
seconded by:_____
carried? Y N

motion made_____
_____

approval moved by:_____
seconded by:_____
carried? Y N

Continued

FIGURE 5-2 *Continued*

motion made_____

_____ _____

approval moved by:_____

seconded by:_____

carried? Y N

motion made_____

_____

approval moved by:_____

seconded by:_____

carried? Y N

New business:

motion made_____

_____

approval moved by:_____

seconded by:_____

carried? Y N

motion made_____

_____

approval moved by:_____

seconded by:_____

carried? Y N

Continued

FIGURE 5-2 *Continued*

motion made_____

_____

approval moved by:_____
seconded by:_____
carried? Y N_____

motion made_____

_____

approval moved by:_____
seconded by:_____
carried? Y N

motion made_____

_____

approval moved by:_____
seconded by:_____
carried? Y N

Adjournment:

moved by:_____
seconded by:_____
carried? Y N

Minutes recorded by:_____

minutes of our library board meetings will make lively reading for future library directors and trustees!

The minutes of the meeting should be sent to library trustees just as they appear in the minutes book, but for other municipal authorities an abbreviated summary is best. I keep the abbreviation down to a page or less and state the items one by one and what action the board took. In this instance, I do not try to provide flavor or interest for city officials. For example, this is the abbreviated summary of the minutes of the fall board meeting at Anytown, which was sent to the city council and mayor:

Minutes of the Anytown Library Board
Regular meeting: September 15, 1991.

Trustees present: Smith, Jones, King, Peterson, Johnson, McTaggert, Houlahan.

Trustees absent: Beugan, Adams.

President Smith called the meeting to order.

The minutes of the June 12, 1991 meeting were approved as read.

Bills amounting to $23,478.31 were presented and approved.

An offer to donate a doll collection to the Anytown Library was referred to the operations committee for study.

The library director's report was approved.

Dr. Peterson reported that the ways and means committee had met and begun preliminary work on the library budget for FY1993.

The Board rejected a proposal to add a second telephone line to the library.

The lack of parking spaces for library users was discussed, but no action was taken.

President Smith appointed the standing committees for the 1991-92 year.

A report on the summer reading program showed that 400 children participated and 297 earned reading certificates for reading ten books or more.

The nonresident fee for library users was increased to $25 per year effective immediately.

The Board voted to raise all pages to minimum wage on January 1, 1992.

Reciprocal borrowing privileges were granted to patrons from the West Creek and Washington Public Libraries within the County.

Use of volunteers in the Anytown Library was discussed.

The meeting was adjourned.

Note that even though the board did not take action on all items on the agenda, mention of each one is made. It is important to know that something was discussed by the board even though a conclusion may not have been reached. The abbreviated minutes are copied and sent to each member of the city council and the mayor. Only the barest facts are given because most people who are not on the library board, and therefore not vitally concerned with the progress of the Anytown Library, will not bother to read through the unedited minutes of the board meeting.

The full minutes of the board meeting are sent to the library trustees first for their perusal. After the library board has had an opportunity to review the minutes of the meeting and raise any questions they might have, the abbreviated minutes are sent to city officials and a press release is written for the media. If significant progress was made at the meeting and a number of changes and/or improvements in policy made, it is a good idea to deal with the items as separate news releases rather than combining them all in one story. An article on Annabel Foster's offer to donate her doll collection to the Library can form the basis of an interesting story even though the board has not taken any action on the matter yet. Increasing the nonresident fee is another board action which warrants its own story, or it could be grouped with the reciprocal borrowing agreement since the two items are somewhat related. Another story could be written combining other items from the meeting like the director's report, the report of the summer reading program, and the discussion on lack of parking for library patrons. Library publicity is essential to help promote usage and the more stories one can send to the media, the more exposure the library will receive. Three stories in place of a single press release about the meeting will improve the image of the library in the community.

SUMMARY

Library board meetings can be made productive for the library by properly preparing for the meetings, educating the trustees about the library, encouraging full board participation, and following up on board decisions. Library directors must work cooperatively with their library boards if they are to raise the quality of their library to acceptable standards of excellence.

ENDNOTES

1. State Standards Commitee, Des Moines, IA. *In Service to Iowa: Public Measures of Quality,* 2nd ed. State Library of Iowa, 1989. p. 7.

2. John K. Brilhart, *Effective Group Discussion.* 5th ed. Dubuque, IA: William C. Brown, 1986. p. 58.

3. Brilhart, p. 76.

4. Lorraine M. Williams, "Fostering Human Values on a Library Board," *Canadian Library Journal,* August 1986: 256.

5. Brilhart, p. 77.

6. Brilhart, p. 76.

7. Charles Hobbs, "Improving Meetings," *Library Administrator's Digest* XXIII, No. 9, November 1988: 67.

8. Brilhart, p. 57.

9. Michael C. Thomsett, *The Little Black Book of Business Meetings.* New York: American Management Association, 1989. p. 4.

10. Catherine S. Ross and Patricia Dewdney, *Communicating Professionally.* New York: Neal-Schuman Publishers Inc., 1989. p. 137.

11. Ross, p. 146.

12. Thomsett, p. 4.

13. Ross, p. 146.

14. Peter F. Drucker, *The Effective Executive.* New York: Harper and Row, 1967. p. 143.

15. Dr. Robert S. Alvarez suggests that when a library director's recommendations are all accepted by his library board it may mean that the director is not making interesting and challenging proposals for change, and that "it reflects the open-minded cooperation that most library boards provide their administrators" (*The Library Boss: Thoughts on Library Personnel.* p. 173). But, as Verna Pungitore points out in her book *Public Librarianship,* "It is the rare library administrator who has never had a suggested course of action rejected by the board" p. 57.

16. Thomsett, pp. 6-7.

17. As Dr. Alvarez points out in his excellent book on library personnel, the library director only rarely receives any praise for his performance from his trustees (*The Library Boss: Thoughts on Library Personnel,* p. 43).

6 REPORTS

Reports are a valuable tool for the library director. They can be used to educate the board of trustees, the library staff, and the public. They come in many varieties including the periodic report of the library director, the annual report of the library, follow-up reports on policy decisions made by the board, reports which indicate the need for action by the board, and informative reports on various aspects of library operation.

THE NEED FOR REPORTS

As we have seen, educating the board of trustees of one's library is of extreme importance in the policy-making process. An uninformed or undereducated board is at risk when attempting to improve the library and its program by making decisions at board meetings. Therefore, it is imperative that the library director educate the board at every opportunity. Educating trustees enhances their commitment to the library. "An indifferent board spells doom for a library program," as an Alabama library director put it. Writing reports and presenting them at library board meetings is one of the best ways to keep the board informed and interested. I can remember times when my library board adopted policies which turned out to be detrimental to the library; they often did so because they had not been properly informed about the issue at hand. They did not have a good grasp of the facts needed to make an educated decision and reacted, instead, like uninformed lay people.

I believe in writing a report or recommendation for nearly every action I expect the board to make, but beyond that, I often prepare progress reports on various aspects of the library merely to educate the trustees. Sometimes I will remark on a situation at one meeting and follow up on it at the next with a report and recommendation that will allow the board the opportunity to deal with the situation. This procedure has the advantage of preparing the trustees in advance of the meeting at which the decision is to be made, thus giving them the opportunity to think about the matter. Library directors don't like surprises at board meetings, but then neither do library trustees! As a library director from Idaho stated it: "Treat them with respect and expect respect in return. Remember they are the 'boss,' but work toward the attitude of partnership. Don't let them be surprised by someone else—keep them informed."

An hours change is a good example of this educating process.

Suppose the Anytown library director has seen a shift in library use away from Saturday mornings, at the same time noting more and more telephone calls asking what time the library closes on weekday evenings. The conclusion is that a trend away from Saturday morning hours toward later weekday closings should be studied with the possibility of recommending a change in hours of opening to the library board. At the next board meeting, a brief report about the situation informs the board that the director will study the matter and place it on the agenda at the next meeting for discussion. In this way, trustees will know that at the next meeting, there may be a proposal to change the library's hours of opening. They will be able to think about the possibility and, if they care to do so, they may ask around to friends, constituents, and other library users about the matter. The trustees will not be faced with an unanticipated item of business for which they have little or no knowledge on which to base a decision.

The chances are much better that a good decision will be made on the basis of the report because the library board has been forewarned that the problem will be discussed. It has been my experience that hours change proposals (a sensitive area for most trustees) are often tabled or referred to committee when presented without any warning. But by giving your board notice in advance of the meeting where the problem will be discussed, you are giving them the opportunity to do their own research on the matter if they wish to do so. "Trustees must also do homework. Only the most superficial treatment of issues can occur if trustees do not take time to consider agenda items before meetings. Conversely, trustees must require administrators to provide balanced and complete information on issues far enough in advance of meeting dates to give trustees time to consider them."[1]

LIBRARY DIRECTOR'S PERIODIC REPORTS

One of the early items on the agenda at my board meetings is the report of the library director. It summarizes what has happened at the library since the last time the library board met. It is too easy to forget items, so I keep a pad handy and jot down things that happen which I think will be important and interesting to my trustees. I may wish to follow up on the results of some minor action by the board in this report, something small which does not, by itself, justify a follow-up report on the agenda. In the report, I will inform the trustees about significant events at the library as well as the statistical side of things and this report will serve as a convenient way to gauge library progress. This report may also serve to let trustees know about important library developments on the regional, state, and national scenes.

Here is an example of the written part of the quarterly library director's report at the Anytown Public Library:

Library Director's Report: May 8, 1991

It was with deep regret that I accepted Mrs. Nelson's request for early retirement as the Anytown Library's children's librarian this spring. She had been employed in this capacity for nearly 12 years and the department had made great strides during her years of service. She was replaced by Mrs. Nancy Jones, a former teacher at the Anytown Elementary School, who is very capable and has a nice rapport with children. Mrs. Jones has a B.A. degree in education with a minor in library and information science and comes to us very highly recommended.

Use of the library continues to run ahead of the previous year by about ten percent, with a large gain in children's use and a small loss in adult use. Sunday circulation improved after a story in the *Clarion* in March, but it is still lower than we anticipated. Use of the library by students from Anytown Community College has also increased this quarter, and the number of cards purchased by nonresidents has reached an all-time high.

The Library received gifts and memorials amounting to $205 this quarter including a $100 gift to the Library's endowment fund. Total receipts from all sources so far this year have reached $132,455.98.

Parking continues to be a problem for Anytown Library users, especially after 3:30 p.m. on weekdays and on Friday nights when the Moose Club across the street plays bingo. There are times when no spaces are available in the Library's parking lot, and library users have complained about the situation to the clerks at the circulation desk.

The library staff continued to make progress on the video cassette collection. About 50 percent of the purchases have been catalogued and are ready for loan. There are still a few problems to work out before the collection can be made available for public loans, but we anticipate resolving them in the near future.

A reference book study course was begun for all adult staff members in January. You will remember that this course is offered as a way to brush up on reference technique and to acquaint staff members with new additions to the reference book collection.

The Anytown Library began making use of its first volunteer this quarter. Pam Simpson, a former member of the adult services staff, has agreed to work from time to time at the library when we need her. She has begun the time-consuming task of sending information to the State Library about titles in the Anytown Library's adult nonfiction collection for inclusion in the state-wide database to facilitate inter-library loan. We are grateful to Mrs. Simpson for her contribution so far.

Friends of the Library held its annual membership drive in February and I am pleased to report that the group now has nearly 150 members. The flower and plant sale in April generated a profit of $396.20, and the money was given to the library to help defray the cost of new furniture in the children's section of the library.

Following this written portion of the report would be various other reports including a breakdown of all library receipts for the first ten months of the fiscal year; a record of library disbursements for the same period; a report of the endowment fund; and a statistical report containing data on circulation of materials, acquisition of materials, and registered borrowers. Note that the written part of the report will often comment on the statistics which are given later in detailed form.

It is a good idea to follow a standardized form for the library director's report so that the trustees will know what to expect and will be able to make comparisons in their own minds from one report to the next. The reports will also serve as a record of the library and its progress and will be very useful both in generating stories for the media and in preparing the annual report of the library. A cover for the director's reports can be made using a computer.[2]

THE LIBRARY'S ANNUAL REPORT

Much has been written about the annual report of the library and many innovative approaches have been taken in recent years. The annual report to the public for many libraries includes a "gim-mick."[3] Library reports have been printed on grocery bags, bookmarks, and even decks of cards for distribution to library users and nonusers. These approaches are great because they take the library message out into the community. "Every library should produce and energetically distribute an annual report. The annual report communicates the whole library story to those who may be aware of only one or two aspects of the library's operations."[4]

The annual report to the board, however, is a different matter. Again, I recommend a standardized report which covers the same information each year because it is easier for the trustee to understand and to draw comparisons. The annual report of the library at Anytown is an enlarged version of the quarterly director's report. It consists of a written report which summarizes the library's year and may run six to eight double-spaced pages. This is followed by various factual reports: a breakdown of library receipts for the year; library expenditures; the endowment fund; memorials and gifts; any special funds the library may have; and a statistical report giving data on circulation, acquisitions, interlibrary loan, and registered borrowers.

In the receipts report, the data is broken down so that year-to-year comparisons may easily be made. For example, if the library has a copy machine, it will be useful to know how use of the machine is going. Decreased receipts may indicate the need to reduce the fee charged per copy, or perhaps the need for a newer, more versatile machine. Increased receipts might reflect the need for a second copy machine. Perhaps the library increased the fee per copy this year. How did the increase affect profit margins and use?

At the Anytown Library, it was noted after reading the annual report that money generated from the original art rental collection was way down when compared to the previous year. The library board wanted to know why, and this led to a study of the situation. A report was written which showed that the people of Anytown did not want to pay a fee to rent original works of art and were avoiding the collection for that reason. The library board was able to change its policy and eventually eliminated the fee.

The annual report of the library is one which cries out for an illustrated cover. The personal computer has simplified this project and made it possible to prepare a report cover which adequately reflects the inside contents. One year my library's informal goal was to interest more farmers in using the library. Much of our publicity was aimed at the rural community and we sought to add materials to the collections which would interest this community.

Our effort was modestly successful and led to an increase in rural tax funds to support the library. The cover of the annual report of the Library reflected this goal by depicting a farm scene which was generated on our computer. It was important to do this because our report was sent out to all of the governing bodies which financially supported the library including the county board. You may wish to use something other than the words "annual report" on your cover. "Although an annual report focuses on a specific time period, it doesn't have to be titled 'annual report.' For many persons these words carry dreary connotations."[5]

The use of graphics in the library's annual report helps to break up page after page of prose. If you decide to use charts and graphs it is a good idea to keep them simple. As they become more complex, the number of people who will understand them decreases. Simple graphics are also easier to design and reproduce. "Pie charts and percentage bar charts are about equally functional for portraying divisions of 100 percent. The bar chart is generally easier to design."[6] Graphics perform another useful function in that one can present a great deal of numerical data in a small space which can be understood at a glance. It is a good way to clarify relationships and is time-saving for the reader of the annual report because it simplifies statistics by making them more concise and condensed in the visual form.[7]

Just as with other library reports, the annual report of the library can be a great source of newspaper and other media publicity and public relations. My time sequence on the annual report is to present it to the library board first. Then, after they have formally approved it and been given the opportunity to add to it or make corrections, I send a copy to each governmental body which supports the library as well as circulate it to the library staff. For our two largest supporters, the city and the county, I make sure that I send individual copies to each member of the boards as well as to the mayor and city manager.

After they have received their copies of the annual report, I mail the entire report to the local media sources. Government officials appreciate getting the opportunity to see the library's annual report before it is released to the public. I've found that by sending the entire report to the media, the coverage often reflects a slant different than the one I would have used had I written a press release based on the report rather than just releasing the report to the media. In our situation this includes two newspapers and a radio station. We also send courtesy copies to the regional and state libraries and to the local chamber of commerce. Other copies are kept in reserve because past experience has shown that city officials will read through the report and then discard it, only to ask me for another one later in the year when they find that they need it for some purpose. One copy is retained and bound for historical purposes. The librarian before me did not bother to keep annual reports (and may not have even written them), so the history and progress of our public library prior to my tenure is virtually lost. All we have are very scanty bits of information from the minutes of board meetings. Binding our annual reports ensures that this will not happen in the future.

What should one do when the past year for the library has been a negative one? My feeling is that you should report both the bad and the good in the annual report. Don't gloss over negatives by overemphasizing the good things that happened at the library. If the budget was slashed, report it and show how the cuts affected the library and its programs. Keep in mind that the annual report of the library is just that—a report of what the library accomplished and what it failed to accomplish in the year just passed. I also use the annual report to make my library board look good. Policy decisions made by the board which resulted in improvements for the library are emphasized, giving credit to the trustees. It would be good to keep in mind the thoughts of a library director from Maine who stated the following: "I remind myself that the trustees are well-intentioned and intelligent and that they are giving of their time to help make the library the best it can be." Directors need to reciprocate by publicly acknowledging the contributions they make as library trustees.

The statistical part of my annual report compares this year to the previous year in terms of circulation, but gives current data only on acquisitions and borrower registration. Much attention has been given in recent years to the efficacy of comparing library circulation from one year to the next but, because this is one of the few comparative statistics kept over the years by most libraries, I believe it is an important measurement tool.[8] The argument is often heard that just because circulation is down it does not necessarily mean that library use is declining. It is true that a library serves people in ways other than by just circulating materials, but that does not reduce the usefulness and reliability of circulation comparisons from one year to the next.[9] Circulation is a concept that the trustee can relate to and it is, in my opinion, still the most important measure of library use in the community. The Anytown Public Library's statistical section of its annual report last year is shown in Figure 6-1.

Because the Anytown Library serves a diverse population and all groups except the populus of the city support the library by

FIGURE 6-1   Statistical Section of the Annual Report

ANYTOWN PUBLIC LIBRARY:
Statistical Report for FY1989

I. CIRCULATION OF MATERIALS

Adult Department	FY1988:	FY1989:	Gain/loss:
nonfiction	26,857	27,967	+1,110
fiction	39,990	39,583	-407
records	1,225	1,058	-167
periodicals	11,141	9,809	-1,332
pictures	39	20	-19
art works	545	329	-216
audio cassettes	131	251	+120
vertical files	301	375	+74
8-track tapes	26	17	-9
films	69	90	+21
filmstrips	6	6	0
a/v equipment	87	86	-1
typewriters	28	0	-28
interlibrary loans out	1,216	1,212	-4
interlibrary loans in	102	156	+54
videocassettes	8	257	+249
Sub-totals:	81,779	81,216	-563

Children's Department	FY1988:	FY1989:	Gain/loss:
nonfiction	8,426	9,622	+1,196
fiction	36,950	44,076	+7,126
periodicals	192	103	-89
records	783	655	-128
audio cassettes	2,007	2,370	+363
filmstrips	172	175	+3
Sub-totals:	48,530	57,001	+8,471
Grand Total:	130,309	138,217	+7,908

contract, it is important to the board to have a breakdown of noncity circulation. So a subsection of this report breaks down the same statistics by residence, and a percentage of total use is computed. This part of the statistical report is shown in Figure 6-2.

Because circulation is broken down by individual items and place of residence, the library board is given the raw data it needs not only to compare the current year to the previous year, but also to see which areas of the collections are being used and which are not. This information can be very useful at budget planning time. The residence circulation statistics are useful in determining the level of funding to support the use being made by residents of a particular area. As we see, for example, rural use of the Anytown Library in FY1989 was 16.53% of total use. The trustees immediately wanted to know how this compared with the amount of money received from the county to pay for this use. It was easy for them to turn back to the receipts report and see that the county had contributed a little over 15 percent of the Library's total budget in FY1989. Acquisition of materials for the Anytown Library is found in the third section of the statistical report shown in Figure 6-3.

You have the option of going into as much detail statistically as you think is required for the education of your library board. At one time at the Carroll Library, I broke down acquisition data to include every item added to the Library, including nonfiction by Dewey decimal 100s. While my library board found the information to be interesting, it was obvious that knowing how many books on literature or history were added during the year was not really very necessary, so we simplified the acquisitions information into broad areas.

A fourth section of the Anytown Public Library's annual statistical report shows information on registered borrowers (Figure 6-4). These statistics are helpful in determining use of the Anytown Library by the diverse groups it serves.

The annual report can also be used to list the names of trustees and staff. This is important because it recognizes a group of people who often receive little or no publicity for tasks accomplished and it gives you a record of names for future years. It makes my task easier when I need to know which trustees served on the board at a particular time and when certain staff members were employed by the library. I usually place this information inside the front cover listing the trustees, their offices, and the committees they head or serve on, followed by the current list of staff members with their job titles.

As to the mechanics of producing the annual report, the comput-

FIGURE 6-2   Circulation by Residence

II. CIRCULATION BY RESIDENCE

	FY1989:	% of Total:
Adult rural	12,120	8.77%
Children's rural	10,726	7.76%
Total rural contract:	22,846	16.53%
Contracting towns	8,074	5.84%
Nonresident college	1,090	.79%
Nonresident paid	7,362	5.33%
Contracting libraries	1,200	.86%
Total other:	17,726	12.82%
Total noncity:	40,572	29.35%

FIGURE 6-3   Acquisition of Materials

III. ACQUISITION OF MATERIALS

	Acquired:	Withdrawn:	Total in the Collection:
Adult section	2,367	701	35,669
Children's section	640	211	11,443
Totals:	3,007	⁻912	47,112

er and copy machine have taken nearly all of the drudgery out of it. I keep a disk just for the annual report. It contains the previous year's written and data reports so I know, by scanning the disk, what reports I will need this year. The forms are there for receipts, disbursements, the memorial fund, the endowment fund, the special funds, and the statistics reports. All I will have to do is change the dates, check the items to see that they are still the same, and replace the old data with the new. The written director's review of the year will have to be rewritten, of course, but I can draw upon reports presented to the library board throughout the year for the ideas. Just as I use different colors of paper in my proposals and reports to the library board at board meetings, I use different colors of paper in the annual report. The cover will reflect the year as closely as possible and I will use at least one chart or graph to break up the written part of my report. The end result is a pleasing, colorful report which my trustees will usually retain and use to compare library progress from one year to the next.

The data in this standardized report can be used as a basis for an eye-catching report to the public. It is here that the library director's ingenuity and flair for the unusual comes into play. The primary audience for the library's annual report includes the library trustees and those government officials who control the

FIGURE 6-4   Registered Borrowers

IV. REGISTERED BORROWERS

City of Anytown	4,555
County borrowers	987
Contracting towns	542
Reciprocal borrowers	405
Nonresident college	167
Nonresident paid	53
Total:	6,709

monetary support for the Library.[10] At the same time, however, the library must seek the widest distribution possible because the annual report contains much information which is of interest to the public.[11]

FOLLOW-UP REPORTS ON BOARD DECISIONS

Some of the policies the library board adopts will require follow-up reports. I try to keep these reports as brief as possible and as unbiased as I can. Without always agreeing with the policy decisions the board makes, I do try to be objective in reporting the results of these decisions. This is very important and serves to underline my working relationship with the board. As a library director from Alabama put it: "Keep them informed, suggest needed policy, present both sides—*never* indicate to staff or public that you feel they made a poor choice." A board is often quite curious to know how their policy decisions turn out. A simple report after three to six months of operation is a good way to supply feedback and help them better understand the implications of their decisions.

If you can keep the report down to one or two pages, all the better. One year the Anytown Library Board, reacting to a difficult parking situation for library users, asked the city to restrict parking in the library's lot to one hour. The city council agreed that the situation needed a solution, but was unwilling to limit parking to one hour and instead put up signs with a two-hour limit. This obviously required a follow-up report to the board.

The staff of the Anytown Library waited until the new signs were up, then gave it a month of operation. At the end of that time they began to gather their data. They asked patrons who came to the library at busy times if they had had any difficulty in finding a parking space. A staff member went outside at different times on different days and observed the parking lot to see if the new policy was having any positive effect and if the city was enforcing the time limit. The following report was presented to the library board:

Follow-Up Report on Limited Parking

Introduction: At its regular meeting in January the Trustees of the Anytown Library voted to ask the city to restrict parking in the lot adjacent to the building to a one-hour limit. The city manager responded by asking the council to limit parking in the library's lot to a two-hour limit, citing two hours as being more consistent with other parking limitations in the city.

Results: Staff members of the Anytown Library took turns

checking the lot during times of peak library use and persons using the library were asked if they had easily found parking spaces near the building. Conclusions drawn from this survey showed little or no improvement in parking accessibility for library users. People are still using the library's parking lot while they do business in the area. While the city does enforce the two-hour limit, few cars parked in the lot remain there longer than two hours, so the policy has had little or no effect in correcting the parking availability problem for the library. Most patrons queried about finding a spot near the building answered that they had not been able to find a place in the lot and had had to park quite some distance from the library.

Conclusion: The parking problem for users of the Anytown Public Library has not been solved. Most library users are still unable to find a parking space in close proximity to the building. It is quite possible that the Board's handling of the problem would have resulted in more positive results had the city not modified its decision and extended the limit to two hours. The parking problem for the Anytown Public Library remains unsolved at this time.

Note that the introduction refreshes the memories of the trustees about the problem and the board's policy decision. You might consider quoting the policy decision directly from the minutes and placing it in the introduction in its entirety. The report is kept as brief as possible without losing its clarity. The conclusion states in a factual way that the problem really hasn't been solved at all. This is a progress report on a policy decision. The board may wish to reopen the discussion and try to arrive at a different solution or it may table it for a future meeting. It may even decide that it can do nothing more about the problem, but at least the trustees will have a better understanding, as a result of this report, of their decision and how it affected the library and its users.

THE ACTION REPORT

A different type of report presented to the library board is one that recommends policy action. The library board members will rely on the library director to inform them of the need for a policy decision and, in most instances, they will expect a recommendation from the director. An Ohio library director explains: "I attempt to be forthright but also realize that our trustees must never be placed in an embarrassing position. They all identify strongly with the library and its success, and seek to strengthen the reasons for their continued identification. They expect me to warn them of potential pitfalls of board policy positions, yet they still support 'freedom of access and information to all.' I believe in strong and continued action in my profession, so the library moves strongly ahead."

Note that in the report on the Anytown Library's parking problem, the library director did not make a specific recommendation. He merely reported the results of a previous board decision, and even though that decision did not solve the problem, the library director left possible additional action up to the board. The action report is different because it makes a recommendation which demands a policy decision from the board.

The Anytown Public Library had a reciprocal borrowing agreement with the other five public libraries in the Anytown area. Through this agreement, persons who had cards at the other libraries were able to use the Anytown Library without charge and Anytown citizens could use the other libraries on the same basis. Anytown had the largest of the six libraries. It was so large, in fact, that it contained more volumes than the other five libraries combined. As might be expected, in a situation of this type, many people from the other five towns used the Anytown Library, but few from Anytown used the resources and services of the other libraries. Why should they when the Anytown Library had the biggest and best program and collections?

It wasn't long after the reciprocal borrowing agreement went into effect that a curious situation began to develop. People from the other five towns began using the Anytown Library exclusively—they didn't even bother trying their own libraries first to see if the materials they needed were available there. "Why should we bother going to two libraries when we know that Anytown has everything we need," they reasoned. But many of the materials they borrowed from the Anytown Library *were* available on the shelves of their own libraries, and Anytown citizens were being deprived of materials bought for their use because they were frequently out on loan to people from the other towns. The library director at Anytown recognized this as an unfair and unhealthy situation and presented the following action report to the Anytown Library Board:

*Report on the Reciprocal Borrowing Agreement
Between Libraries*

Introduction: In 1981, the Anytown Public Library entered into a reciprocal borrowing agreement with the other five public libraries in the area. Under the terms of this agreement, each public library agreed to loan its materials to citizens of the other five towns without charge. One provision of the agreement stated that it could be terminated at any time by any party to the agreement. In the eight years during which the agreement has been in effect, use of the Anytown Public Library by people from the other five towns has increased steadily.

The Present Situation: Use of the Anytown Public Library during FY1989 by persons living in the towns covered by the reciprocal borrowing agreement reached 8,074 circulation units. Over 400 people living in these towns have applied for library cards at the Anytown Public Library. We have not been able to find anyone in the Anytown community who has a library card at any of the other libraries and the librarians in those towns have refused to provide us with this information.

The names of people residing in the towns consistently appear on reserve lists for books and other materials popular with Anytown Library users. Many of our nonresident users have told library staff members that they use the Anytown Public Library in preference to their own because of its wide range of materials and depth of collections. In visiting with the other five librarians it was learned that four of them feel they are losing patrons to the Anytown Library and are not happy with the reciprocal borrowing agreement.

Recommendation: Because the reciprocal borrowing agreement between the six public libraries in the Anytown area has not led to use of all libraries by all citizens but has resulted in heavy use of the Anytown Public Library, often at the expense of the other libraries, I recommend that the reciprocal borrowing agreement be discontinued and residents of the five towns currently covered by this agreement be treated like all other nonresidents not covered by service contracts.

A copy of the actual reciprocal borrowing agreement would appear as an appendix to this report. Note that the recommendation from the library director is a very specific one and this is important. It may not lead to a decision by the board which reflects the director's recommendation, but the trustees will know exactly how the director assesses the situation and what policy he feels should be adopted. Again, the report is kept as brief as possible while still conveying all of the needed facts. The director's bias is held to a minimum. The first paragraph goes back to the minutes of the board when the reciprocal borrowing agreement is adopted. The exact passage may be quoted, if necessary, and this refreshes some of the trustees' memories about the situation and introduces the information to those trustees who may not have been a part of the board when the decision was reached. The action report relates information about a situation which affects the library and makes a recommendation to rectify that situation.

THE INFORMATION REPORT

A report I use frequently with my library board is one I call "the information report." It is merely a way of informing the board about a topic of concern or interest in the library, and it requires no action on the part of the trustees. Its sole purpose is to educate the board. A good example of this type of report at the Anytown Public Library is one prepared concerning the use of the periodicals collection. Here is the report:

The Magazine and Newspaper Collections at the Anytown Public Library

Introduction: The Anytown Public Library subscribes to 168 magazines and newspapers. Back issues are retained for a period of ten years and may be borrowed by library patrons. A recent survey of periodical use was conducted by the Anytown Library staff. This report was prepared to acquaint members of the library board and staff with the operation and use of this resource.

Selection and Ordering of Titles: The main criterion for selecting magazines for the collection is whether or not they are indexed in the unabridged *Reader's Guide To Periodical Literature.* Since the Anytown Library subscribes to this index, use of the collection, particularly back issues, is related to the availability of a standard index to magazine articles.

The Reader's Guide indexes about 200 magazines. The Anytown Public Library subscribes to 145 of them. The 145 subscriptions were selected for inclusion in the collection by a trial-and-error process. Some subscriptions were tried for one year and eliminated because they did not circulate to Anytown users. Others were not included because they affect tastes not commonly found in Anytown (*Motor Boating & Sailing* for example).

Other titles that are not indexed in *Reader's Guide* are selected because they reflect special interests of the people served by the library (*Soybean Digest, National Hog Farmer,* and *Farmer's Digest* are examples). Still other titles were purchased because of special requests by patrons (*Golf Digest* and *Runner's World*).

The Anytown Library also subscribes to 13 newspapers including all four printed in Anytown County, the three major cities near Anytown and several national newspapers like *The Wall Street Journal, USA Today,* and *The Christian Science Monitor.*

Subscriptions are renewed each year through the Acme Subscription Agency where the Library receives a ten percent discount on the total invoice. A few magazines and newspapers are ordered and renewed through the publishers.

Periodical Display and Storage: The Anytown Library has shelving space to display only 100 magazines and newspapers for reading in the library. The remaining titles are kept at the circulation desk and may be borrowed for use in the reading room. A list of these magazines is displayed prominently near the lounge area. Back issues of magazines are retained by the Anytown Library for a period of ten years and back issues of newspapers are kept for a six-month period. The Anytown Clarion is received on microfilm and the Library has issues of this newspaper and its predecessors back to 1863.

Use of the Periodical Collection: Older issues of magazines and newspapers may be borrowed for the same two-week period which applies to books and other materials. The main users of the back issues of the library's magazines are students at the high school and community college. Our survey of magazine circulation showed that 95% of the use was student use. Newspapers are not borrowed very often; they are used primarily in the reading room. Back issues of the *Anytown Clarion* on microfilm are used by adults for local history and genealogy research, and by students for special assignments. The microfilm is used very frequently and, at times, there are people waiting to use the library's only machine. Adults make the most use of current issues of magazines in the reading lounge area.

Our survey showed heavy borrowing of the news magazines with *Newsweek, Time,* and *U.S. News & World Report* being used the most. Homemaking magazines are also popular with *Better Homes & Gardens, Ladies Home Journal,* and *Country Woman* leading the list. Sports magazines like *Bicy-*

cling, Sports Illustrated, and *Runner's World* have a strong following, and the farming magazines are also borrowed frequently.

Summary: The periodicals collection of the Anytown Public Library is a popular one. One hundred and sixty-eight magazines and newspapers make up the core collection and are available to library users for reading in the Library and to take home.

There are several things to notice about this report. First of all, it minimizes the use of library jargon. Most trustees feel more comfortable speaking English rather than "librarianese." The only word in this report the least bit technical is "periodical," and it might be a good idea to explain to the trustees that the term was used only because it was easier when referring to both magazines and newspapers. Don't be afraid to use common everyday terms when reporting on the library. Your trustees will appreciate it.

It is useful to have both an introduction and a summary, for it ties the report together and leaves the trustees with a message. I am always amazed at how much information my trustees glean from my reports and later use in their decisions concerning the library. The report is kept brief and to the point. This report contains concise information—it informs without becoming so lengthy that it bores.

Note also that this report plants an idea in the trustees' minds for possible future action. In the paragraph on "Use of the Periodical Collection," the library director states that use of the *Anytown Clarion* on microfilm is very heavy. This may later be referred to in a proposal to purchase a second microfilm reader for the Anytown Library, or to purchase an even more expensive item, a microfilm/fiche reader/printer. In a proposal at a later meeting the director may say that "You will remember in my report on the periodicals collection that use of the microfilm has been heavy," and then build on that statement in the proposal. Occasionally, the trustees will pick up on the idea you have planted and suggest at the same meeting that the project be instigated, but most of the time they will not.

There are an infinite number of information reports which can be written and presented to one's library board. Remember, your purpose is to educate the trustees so that they will make more intelligent policy decisions in the future. They need to know all about library operation, and the more information you can feed them, the better the chances are that you will be able to improve the library. They may offer some suggestions or tips on improving the procedures you employ. This is often helpful and the wise library director will not resent this kind of intrusion into library administration. A library director from Nova Scotia explained her philosophy as follows: "I feel that we are all working for the good of the library. We may disagree about certain points; however each one is sincere. I believe the board is there to help me, and sometimes they have saved me from moving in a wrong direction when I got carried away with a 'grand scheme.'"

One of the most effective information reports I ever presented to my trustees was one on book selection. I always assumed that my trustees knew how materials were selected for the library but, as it turned out, they didn't have the foggiest idea how the process worked. They were very pleased to be enlightened and have often thanked me for showing them, in reports, how the library functions.

PRESENTATION OF REPORTS

Committee reports tend to be more detailed than reports presented to the full board. One of the reasons this is true is that the committee deals with a limited range of business—often just one item, as in the case of a ways and means committee studying the annual budget for the library. As we have seen, an agenda is essential for a library-related meeting whether it is a meeting of a committee, of the full board, or of an auxiliary group like the friends of the library. The report must be listed on the agenda and the agenda sent to the members prior to the meeting.

I find it unsatisfactory to distribute most reports ahead of time. There are exceptions to this rule, as in the case of making wage and salary recommendations to the ways and means committee. Committee meetings tend to be shorter than board meetings. For this reason and the fact that I want to give the committee the opportunity to study and research wage and salary proposals ahead of time, I will send out a copy of my report a couple of days before the meeting. In a cover letter, all committee members are encouraged to read through the report, which is very brief—often only a page or two. In nearly every instance, when dealing with wage and salary proposals, committee members will have read the material before the meeting and will already have formulated questions regarding the recommendations.

For the full board, however, I will only send out a report prior to the meeting if we are dealing with a complicated issue which requires homework. Nearly all other reports, while listed by descriptive title on the agenda mailed out to every trustee, will be read through, by me, at the meeting. It does not work very well to have each trustee read through the report silently because reading speeds and comprehensions differ from trustee to trustee. The library director can read through the report slowly and amplify passages as he goes along, if necessary. This will usually result in nearly complete comprehension of the points being made.

A time for discussion should follow each report even though it may be the type of report which requires no board action. For longer reports, it is helpful to list the items covered in the report on the last page or on a separate sheet to stimulate discussion. Communication plays a vital role in the presentation of reports to the library board. A library director in British Columbia commented: "I believe in common courtesy and in the effective use of communication skills—listening well, speaking clearly, showing positive and nonthreatening body language, and writing succinctly. I strive to deliver good service and to make my board look good."

USING REPORTS FOR THE MEDIA

Reports about the library which are used to inform and educate the board are also great resources for educating the library's public. Obviously, they must be presented to the library board first but, after that, they can be used to write publicity for and about the library. Just as most library board members are somewhat uninformed concerning the function and operation of the public library, so also is the general public.

In most instances, it is useful to base a written press release done by a library staff member on the report itself rather than releasing the report to the media. This will vary, of course, from community to community. I have found that releasing a report to the newspaper is a gamble. Sometimes, as in the case of the annual report which goes directly to the newspaper's editor who is a friend of mine, this gamble will pay off and the resulting news item will be great publicity for the library. But on other occasions, the result will be almost total misinformation and I will lie awake at night wondering how they could write *that* story on the basis of the information I provided.

At one time, when the publisher of the local newspaper was a member of my library board and his paid staff was small, I could write a story about any aspect of the library and it would appear verbatim in the newspaper. I was a young and inexperienced library director at the time and assumed that this was the way it would always be. Alas, the day soon came when my trustee was no longer in charge and every press release I wrote about the library was completely rewritten by a newspaper staff member who often destroyed or warped the original meaning I had intended to convey. For years, I fumed about the unfairness and stupidity of this practice, but it never changed. Stories about library board meetings appeared in the newspaper emphasizing some minor point while major policy decisions were totally excised from the story.

As the years have rolled by, I've come to the conclusion that bad library publicity is better, by far, than no publicity at all. Getting the library's name before the public is vital, so I continue to take my reports and recommendations to the library board and later rewrite them for the media. Many of my stories will not appear because the editor thinks they are not "newsworthy." But sometimes just the hint that the library may produce its own newsletter and not release its stories to the media is enough to cause reconsideration of a library press release.

Library newsletters are a viable approach to library publicity, however, because the director can control the content of each story and at the same time make sure it gets into the hands of an interested person. But while newspaper and radio publicity reaches a wide audience, the library newsletter tends to fall into the hands of people who are already confirmed library users, so both approaches are needed.

SUMMARY

Reports written by the library director and presented to the library board are needed to educate the library trustees. Periodic reports on the state of the library, annual reports, follow-up reports on board decisions, action reports with specific recommendations, and strictly information reports all combine to provide the library board with the information it needs to develop sound, imaginative, and knowledgeable policies for improving the adequacy of the library. An informed board is a productive board. Reports can be presented to committees and full library boards and also can be used to generate press releases for the media.

ENDNOTES

1. William Amundson with Milton Mitchell, "The Policy Making Role of the System Trustee," *Wisconsin Library Bulletin,* Spring, 1984: 25.

2. Graphics software offers an easy way to use the computer to prepare attractive report covers.

3. See various issues of *The Library Administrator's Digest* by Dr. Robert S. Alvarez. South San Francisco, CA: Administrator's Digest Press.

4. Kathleen K. Rummel and Esther Perica, eds. *Persuasive Public Relations.* Chicago: American Library Association, 1983. p. 154.

5. Rummel, p. 155.

6. B.Y. Auger, *How To Run More Effective Business Meetings.* New York: Grosset and Dunlap, 1964. p. 116.

7. Catherine S. Ross and Patricia Dewdney, *Communicating Professionally.* New York: Neal-Schuman Publishers, Inc., 1989. p. 70.

8. ". . .statements that a library's circulation 'is not a measure of satisfaction or quality service' will always surprise me. It may not be the only measure but certainly it is a measure. And we believe that for the time being, it is the best single measure that we have in public libraries." Dr. Robert S. Alvarez in *The Library Boss: Thoughts on Library Personnel.* South San Francisco, CA: Administrator's Digest Press, 1987. p. 80.

9. ". . .circulation normally goes up when people are satisfied with the quality of service, and goes down when the quality drops off. The correlation between the variables here is quite high. When the expected relationship is not there, one can be fairly sure that the answer lies in outside economic conditions that are beyond the control of the librarian." Alvarez, p. 80.

10. Rummel, p. 154.

11. Rummel, p. 157.

7 COMMUNICATION

Effective communication is the cornerstone in any successful library director/library board relationship. The library board must know at all times what the library director needs and wants for the library. At the same time the library director needs to listen to the trustees and consider their ideas seriously. Honesty is critical in all relationships with library trustees, and there is no room for a policy of telling the board only what you want them to know or only what you think they *need* to know. Effective communication is based on full disclosure of *all* the facts and will lead to a more productive relationship between board and director.

EVENHANDED TREATMENT

Most library directors can attest to the fact that some library trustees are more interested in the library, its collections, programs, and progress than others. It only stands to reason that the level of interest in the library by those selected to provide for library improvement will vary from individual to individual. Time and energy availability are important considerations. A library trustee who is retired or works regular hours will have more time available for the library and board than someone like a physician or factory worker who may work on an irregular schedule with overtime hours.

Because this is true, it is always a temptation for the library director to give preferential treatment to those trustees who express an interest. Mavis Johnson was one of those trustees at the Anytown Public Library. She nearly always supported the library director at board meetings and used the services of the library extensively without asking for special favors. Mavis was always out in the community encouraging people to use the library and boasting about what a wonderful asset the library was to Anytown. So, when the library director was notified by a national foundation that the library's grant proposal for funding an index to the Anytown Clarion newspaper—a project Mavis had championed—had been approved, it was very tempting for the library director to tell her the good news first. Instead, a memo was prepared and mailed to *every* library trustee, even Ebenezer McTaggart who had opposed the grant in the first place telling everyone who would listen that it was a waste of time and money. The principle at work here is to treat all trustees equally because *they are equal*. Each trustee has one vote on the board and each trustee needs to know that that vote is just as powerful as that of any other trustee, including the officers and those trustees who head committees.

There will be times when the library director cannot control the flow of information about a topic concerning the library. Trustees will be given advance information occasionally, and will pass that information along to other trustees (the library director may be the last one to know!). Still, the library director must be fair and judicious in communicating knowledge to the library board members. My board, for example, meets regularly on a quarterly basis, and others may be called when needed. There are items of concern to the library which come up between meetings, items which don't warrant the calling of a special meeting, but do need to be communicated to members of the board. I avoid, at all costs, informing only certain members of the board, but try to let everyone know at the same time. By telephoning I would be allowing the first person I call to immediately call another trustee before I can do so. It seems preferable that each member of the library board hear the news from me and I believe that a written communication is the best way to reach this goal.

There are times when equal communication to all trustees is difficult to achieve. What do you do when the board president calls and pumps you for information that should be released to all the board? You may be able to say that you will be releasing that information to everyone in the form of a memo, but not every board president will accept that answer. If the item is forced into the open and you need to tell one member of the board, you should send out a memo to all members as soon as possible. Because of the committee structure of the library board, there will sometimes be information in the hands of some trustees and not in the hands of others and there is little the library director can do to prevent this. It is important, however, to not reveal information in committee which should be released to all trustees. Committee members do not always stay on track at their meetings, and curious or interested trustees will often question the library director about other items of information concerning the library. I try to talk my way out of releasing library news, if at all possible, but sometimes it is unavoidable.

Another source of irritation for library trustees is to read in the local media information they should have been privy to first. I always make certain that my letter to the library board goes out and has had a chance to be read by each trustee *before* I release the same news to the media. This is communication and it is vital that the board be informed at the outset. It is important for the library director to be in control of the library's publicity and I discourage trustees from releasing library-related news unless they clear it with me first. Still, there are media items I cannot control, and every now and then our newspaper or radio station picks up an item which concerns our library directly or indirectly from another source, usually the state or regional libraries. When this occurs, I may elaborate on it with a letter to my trustees and let them know that I did not send the story to the media. The library director's goal must always be to communicate library information directly to all trustees at the same time whenever possible. A library director from South Carolina defined her responsibility to communicate with her board this way: "To keep them informed on the library's progress. To involve them on policy decisions and to work with them in promoting the library. I try to have a friendly relationship, without getting too close."

There is a certain amount of psychology at work here. How can we expect the board to function if all members are not kept informed first and on an equal basis? Don't ever decide whether or not a certain trustee needs a bit of information about the library. Each trustee has the same right to know every matter concerning the library and its policies as every other trustee, whether interested or not, whether an officer or not, or whether an active trustee or not. The best way to make a trustee feel inadequate is to slight him or her in the communication process. Remember that: "Effective board/executive relationships begin and end with good communication."[1]

As lay people and library trustees, library board members are expected by their friends and associates to know everything about the library. Trustees serve as a bridge between individuals in the community and the library. In this capacity they need to be kept informed about any and every thing going on at the library.[2] The director of a South Dakota library explains: "The board member is the communication link with the community-at-large and should have a basic knowledge of library policies and procedures and a basic understanding of library questions." "No matter how knowledgeable the trustee, how finely tuned to the community and how well-prepared to discuss a problem, the trustee must rely upon the strength of the library director and staff."[3]

COMMUNICATING AT COMMITTEE MEETINGS

Committee meetings will be successful only if proper groundwork is done—members need to get information before the committee meeting. Committee meetings are different in one respect from meetings of the full board: they tend to concentrate on a limited agenda for a set period of time. Because this is true the library director needs to submit background material to members of the committee before the meeting. Trustees on a standing or special committee will almost always take the time to prepare themselves for a committee meeting. At a meeting of the full board, a member may get away with not having the vaguest idea what is being discussed because of no preparation for the topic, but this is not so easily accomplished when the group is small. I have found that if I send out a reasonable amount of concise material nearly all trustees will sift through it before the committee meets. Questions may arise about the material I send them and an occasional telephone caller before the meeting may be asking for an explanation or clarification, but when the meeting takes place, all of the committee members usually will be prepared to discuss the topic at hand.

Just as with other meetings with trustees, an agenda distributed before the meeting is a must. You need to state the charge from the parent library board to all the members of the committee in this communication in order for them to understand the purpose of the meeting. Don't ever assume that every trustee knows what the meeting is about.

A properly prepared committee should be able to reach a decision within an hour's time. If it cannot do so, a second meeting should be arranged. I feel that if a decision cannot be reached after one hour's discussion, it is better to schedule another meeting rather than risk a bad decision just because the committee members are tired and want to go home. Honest communication is a must at the committee meeting. The trustees will appreciate knowing how the library director feels on matters of mutual concern even though they may not agree with him. Mutual understanding and trust is just one of many positive results of good communication at the committee meeting level.

COMMUNICATING AT BOARD MEETINGS

Your best form of nonverbal communication at a library board meeting is a friendly smile. Trustees should be made welcome at meetings of the board, and it will fall upon the library director to make certain this happens. The serving of food at a board meeting is another way of saying that you appreciate the time and effort library trustees spend for the library and that they are welcome at meetings. A South Carolina library director recommends: "Be honest, be informative and be willing to go the extra mile. Since they are working without pay, be aware of the time and money they are graciously committing to the library and don't overburden them with inconsequential details."

Written communications for the trustees at the board meeting must be concise, to the point, and engagingly written. As library director, you have the obligation to your board of trustees to make the meetings as interesting and enjoyable as possible. You need to provide items on the agenda which will stimulate discussion between you and your board, but also between the trustees themselves. A written communication on any topic needs to be lively. It is not so strange that library trustees, like the rest of us, enjoy a good discussion. You should strive to word your communications in such a way that they encourage discussion at the board meetings. If you present reports and recommendations which are open-ended—that is, they don't appear to be written by a library director who has all the answers—you should be able to initiate productive discussions about the library and its progress. Even a little controversy is better than boredom!

The second meeting of my library board was a very memorable one and at least one of my former trustees who was present at that meeting still remarks about it. The early meetings in a new library director's tenure are often memorable and interesting because the trust and mutual understanding has not yet been established, and many of the new director's ideas are foreign to the library board. At this particular meeting, the board needed to make several important decisions and every trustee attended the meeting. Each item was discussed at length and nearly every trustee had a contribution to make. The meeting went way past its scheduled time and, after adjournment, the president of the board asked me to defend the addition to the library of *Catcher in the Rye* by J.D. Salinger.

Considering the graphic passages in today's novels, it seems almost unbelievable now that a book like *Catcher in the Rye* could be challenged and it caught me totally by surprise. I spent another hour defending my choice of books for the Carroll Library. No one left the meeting even though it lasted until after 11 p.m. My trustees stayed to listen to my defense and contribute their thoughts on the book, the book selection process, and censorship of library materials. It was one of the most interesting board meetings we ever had and everyone enjoyed it thoroughly. At subsequent meetings I tried to include items of business on the agendas which would provoke interesting discussion and communication between the trustees and myself. Surely some degree of intellectual stimulation should reward service on the library board!

Library board meetings do not have to be dull and tedious. If they are, your trustees will find another place to be when the board meets. Effective communication is a skill which can be learned and *needs to be learned* by a library director in order to interact with the library board at meetings. "Good listening is the foundation of all face-to-face communication between people. This is so because communication is not a one-way process of a speaker sending a message to a passive receiver. Communication is a two-way transaction in which the listener as well as the speaker is actively involved."[4]

COMMUNICATING BETWEEN MEETINGS

It is important to keep in touch with library board trustees when the committees and board are not meeting. You may continue to educate and enlighten them about the library in person, on the telephone, and through the mail. Try to be in contact with your trustees at all times. Your relationship with the board president, heads of committees, and individual trustees should be friendly enough that you can call on them when you need help. Do you have this sort of relationship with your board, or do you feel uncomfortable about making contact with trustees at unscheduled times? A library director from South Dakota wrote: "You need to be diplomatic and able to relate to all types of people. Effort must be made to get to know each board member individually and understand their needs. No amount of library knowledge and skills will replace the need for good people skills."

Sending out the minutes of committee or board meetings presents an opportunity for a more personal communication. When I communicate with my trustees by sending them the minutes I sometimes add a personal note. I may follow-up on something said by the trustee or I may thank the person for his support on a matter of concern to me. In this way, I am able to change an impersonal communication (the minutes) into something more personal between us. This is a small way of saying "I appreciate your support of the library and the contributions you make at meetings" and your trustees will be grateful that you took the time for this small courtesy.

Some library directors have told me that they want to maintain a business-only relationship with their library trustees, but I disagree with this idea. I want to create a feeling of mutual concern and understanding between each trustee and myself. To do so, I treat each of them as I would a friend. I send cards when they are sick and flowers when a family member dies. I congratulate them when they do something great and I sympathize with them when things go wrong. Although I don't give them special library favors (and my trustees don't expect them), I give them the best possible library service I can provide. Whenever I write a story for the media, I try to mention the library trustees. I want them to receive credit for the accomplishments they enable the library to make. "The point is that the librarian and the board support one another and are not shy about saying so in public."[5]

As library directors we need to communicate to our boards that they are important for the public library's survival. But we also need to let them know we are a team—we will work together toward a common goal. A director from Louisiana recommends: "Let the board know from the beginning that you want to be responsible for the execution of your job, but with their support. Avoid slipping into the attitude that the board is your superior, because really it is not. You and the board are equals, each with clearly defined, unique duties and responsibilities." At the same time we need to reinforce the idea that "library board members are highly dedicated individuals committed to excellent public library service."[6] We must remember that in a very real sense our trustees are also our public, the very people we are in business to serve.[7]

SUMMARY

Communication between the library director and the library board is essential to the well-being of the library. If the communication process breaks down the library will not be able to reach its potential. It is important to keep the channels of communication open at all times, not just when the board and director have a regularly scheduled encounter. The two must create their own environment of mutual understanding and trust in order to produce the best possible library for the community they serve.

ENDNOTES

1. Diane J. Duca, *Nonprofit Boards: A Practical Guide to Roles, Responsibilities, and Performance.* Phoenix, AZ: The Oryx Press, 1986. p. 147.

2. Robert D. Franklin "The Administrator and the Board," *Library Trends* 11, no. 1, July 1962: 57-58.

3. Alice B. Ihrig, *Decision-Making for Public Libraries.* Hamden, CT: The Shoestring Press, 1989. pp. 41-42.

4. Catherine S. Ross and Patricia Dewdney, *Communicating Professionally.* New York: Neal-Schuman Publishers, Inc., 1989. p. 32.

5. Guy St. Clair and Joan Williamson, *Managing the One-Person Library.* London: Butterworth & Co. (Publishers) Ltd., 1986. p. 34.

6. Irvin H. Sherman, "What Makes a Library Well-Run?" *Canadian Library Journal,* October 1984: 251.

7. Christine Van Roodselaar and Michael Prior, "The Library Trustee: An Alberta Perspective," *Canadian Library Journal,* August 1988: 226.

8 LIBRARY BOARDS AND PUBLIC RELATIONS

There are many areas of library development and improvement which lend themselves to direct participation by library trustees. One of these areas is public relations. Getting the library message out into the community can often be accomplished more effectively by library trustees than by library administrators; better still is a team approach using the strengths of both trustees *and* administrators.

THE PUBLIC RELATIONS COMMITTEE

One of the standing committees of any public library's board of trustees should have the development of a public relations program for the library as one of its functions. This can be accomplished by adding this area of responsibility to one of the standing committees or by forming a special committee to take charge of the program. Trustees bring to this phase of library operation a point of view which is not very far removed from that of the general public and this can be of considerable help in promoting the library in the community. In fact, this point of view is one of the strengths of a public library operating with a governing board of trustees. "Trustees see the library from the public's vantage point. In fact every time they enter the library, they should try to see it as a newcomer sees it."[1] The latter point could also be made for the library director—each time you enter your library try to see it as you would as a stranger entering for the first time.

Public relations for the library will have as its goal to increase usage of the collections, programs, and services offered by the library and to bring in members of the community not currently using the library. "Librarians want their libraries to be used, and the only way to get people to use them is to let them know what they can find at the library."[2]

At one point in my tenure as director of the Carroll Public Library, one of my trustees suggested that the operations committee be renamed to incorporate and emphasize public relations as one of its functions. This was not intended as a criticism of my own PR efforts, but was an honest effort to aid me and to bring a different perspective to the process. I thought it was a great idea partly because I hoped that it would take some of the work load off my shoulders and at the same time bring in some new ideas for publicity. The Library Board agreed with the idea and, after the committee was renamed, it met a few times to map out a year-long public relations campaign.

A development like this can be extremely helpful to the library director, even if the end result is only ideas and not the actual performance of tasks, which is what happened at my library. The committee met and discussed numerous ideas (some old, some new) and eventually decided upon a long list of PR "gimmicks" they wanted *me* to try. The members of this committee did not perceive their role as one actually involved in doing the campaign, but felt they should provide the ideas and the money.

The role of the library board in public relations is that of policy making, not actually running the campaign or program. The trustees should "formulate the basic policies on which the library's public relations program is based."[3] At the Carroll Library several good ideas came out of the PR meetings and committee members persuaded the full board to more than double the amount of money in the library's budget designated for public relations. But as to reducing my PR workload, just the opposite occurred, for they wanted me to continue with my own press releases and other public relations ideas as well as incorporating the ideas the committee had generated!

Some of the best ideas eventually adopted by this committee which found their way to the library board for approval, came from brainstorming or "what-if?" sessions where members tossed out ideas at random, built on others' ideas, and let their imaginations run wild. Brainstorming is a particularly effective technique in generating publicity ideas for the library. Remember that committees by themselves cannot make decisions affecting the library. They may discuss problems and make recommendations to the full board, but the library board reserves the right to make the final decisions and establish policies. The committee may meet frequently and develop a planned public relations program which is then submitted to the library board for approval. Changes in the program frequently occur at the board meeting where ideas, which seemed so wonderful at the committee meeting, receive closer scrutiny.

It is best for a committee charged with developing a public relations program or campaign for the library to meet frequently during a short span of time. Remember that trustees have other interests besides the library and it is easy for them to forget what was discussed at the last meeting. Meeting frequently overcomes this obstacle to a certain extent, but it is also a good idea to write up a summary of ideas discussed at the previous meeting and send it out to committee members and also provide a copy at the next meeting. This will allow committee members to think about the campaign and may even prevent them from reconsidering old ideas. The opening session of a committee meeting to map out a public relations campaign should discuss the meaning of PR. There are many good books available on this subject as it relates to all types of libraries.

THE BOARD AND THE MEDIA

Another strong advantage frequently brought to library public relations by library trustees is their knowledge of effective advertising techniques and their "clout" with the media. Most library boards have at least one member who advertises heavily in the media, and can introduce the library director and the library's mission to the key media people at the newspaper, radio, and television outlets. It is also helpful to have at least one library trustee who is intimately involved in one of the local media sources, particularly the newspaper, if possible. The best years of publicity for our library occurred when the owner and publisher of the *Carroll Times Herald* newspaper was a library trustee.

The library board will only be able to help with library public relations if it has been properly educated by the library director. This concept cannot be repeated often enough for it is only when the board has been thoroughly indoctrinated as to the purposes and functions of the library that it can be an effective agent of change for the library. Nowhere else is this process so apparent as in promoting the library to the community. By educating the library trustees in committee, at board meetings, and between meetings, the library director will enable these key people to understand, interpret, and communicate that which is vital about the library to the community. Your goal, as library director, is to make your library the best it can be and this goal is an integral part of public relations—". . .good public relations for libraries is directed. . .to an enriched quality of service."[4]

Active participation in a library's public relations program by library trustees should be a top priority for the library director. The library board is viewed as a bridge between the community and the library and, as such, should provide for a two-way channel of information—from the community to the library, and from the library to the community. In the words of a Wyoming library director: "These are volunteers who want to do the best job they can. You need to give them the background to do so. They are not, probably, going to live at the library as you do, but they are bright, generally well-informed people who will probably do as you suggest if they trust you." Library trustees are really lay people who have had the opportunity to learn and know more about the library because of their special role on the board. But just because they have been elected or appointed to the position of library trustee does not mean that they have stopped being lay people. They will continue to serve the library out in the community and if they have been properly informed and educated about the library, they will do effective public relations in a liason capacity to and with other lay people. As the library improves and the quality of its resources and services goes up, trustees will communicate that message to the people the library serves by telling them what your library has to offer.[5]

One of the criticisms levelled at library directors is that they fail to involve trustees in the library's program and, in effect, relegate them to an advisory role when they actually are charged with a governing function.[6] The public relations arena is well-suited to trustee participation; trustees have a wealth of talent and experience to offer the library and should be encouraged to contribute. A Michigan library director explained it as follows: "They represent the citizens' viewpoint and we work together to provide good library service to the city. They also are an important part of public relations and reach many segments of the population I may not be able to contact otherwise."

Rita Kohn and Krysta Tepper, in their excellent public relations skills manual for librarians *You Can Do It,* write that library trustees can and should take an active role in the library's ongoing PR program. They write that "because community leaders look to the library board members as the spokespersons of the library, the members will need to be articulate about the operation of the library to the general public and to the mass media. Board members must *be available to appear before any group* for a program, to sit on commissions involved with community growth, to establish the library as a worthy recipient of tax deductible grants, bequests and matching funds. Board members must also be aware of what the mass media is reporting or editorializing about the library and must respond accordingly, either to express appreciation or to correct. ACCEPTANCE OF LEADERSHIP WITHIN THE COMMUNITY is a. . .PR expectation."[7]

PROMOTING THE BOARD IN NEWS RELEASES

Library boards are quite often what I call "hidden boards," that is, they frequently function in a "behind-the-scenes" way so that the members of the board are unknown in this capacity in the community. The fact that someone is a member of the board of trustees of the local public library appears in one's obituary, but all too often that is the only time a trustee's name appears in the newspaper as a member of the library board. Of course, when trouble erupts at the library, trustees names surface in the media, but all too often this is a negative type of recognition.

Names of trustees should appear regularly in press releases written to promote the library. This will yield positive results in terms of pride at being a library trustee. It will also make trustees known as board members in the community, increase public awareness of the library and its programs, and promote communication and input from the public to those who control library policy. Any press release regarding a library board meeting should list the trustees by name and office. This can be done at the end of the article or the names can be placed within the context of the press release.

Public relations is a matter of creating an image. "Everything we do creates an image in someone else's mind. Good or bad, like it or not, we all have public relations. Our job is to create a positive image about the library."[8] We need to include in the image of our library the fact that the library is governed by an active board of trustees who are seeking, at all times, to make the library the best it can be in the community it serves.

Here is an example of a press release written after a meeting of the library board of the Anytown Public Library:

ANYTOWN LIBRARY BOARD ELECTS OFFICERS

At the regular meeting of the Board of Trustees of the Anytown Public Library on Monday evening, September 11, 1991 James Smith was elected president. Other new officers of the board include Frances Houlahan, vice president, and Mavis Johnson, recording clerk. Mr. Smith appointed the board's standing committees as follows: Ways and Means—Dr. Zane Peterson, Felcity Adams, and Johnson; Operations and Public Relations—Dorothy King, Ebenezer McTaggert, and Penelope Jones; and Bylaws/Goals—Mavis Johnson, Houlahan, and John Beugan.

In other business at Monday night's meeting, a proposal for a lighted "hours open" sign was unanimously approved. The sign will be placed near the northeast corner of the library and will be illuminated during evening hours when the Anytown Public Library is open for business. President Smith called the decision to purchase the sign "long overdue," and hoped it would lead to increased use of the Anytown library during the evening hours.

   The library board will meet again on December 11, 1991 at 5:30 p.m. in the Library's meeting room to discuss the Library's operating budget for F1993. Anyone wishing to attend this meeting will be welcome.

A press release announcing an election of officers is obviously a golden opportunity to put the names of all library trustees before the public, but all meetings of the board and its committees should be reported to the media and should list the members somewhere in the body of the article. If the information cannot be worked in unobtrusively, then the members may be included at the end in a paragraph which simply lists them by name.

Other media presentations should also name the members of the board whenever possible. Their names should be listed in the annual report, on brochures produced to help users and nonusers understand the library, in summaries of minutes sent to the various governmental agencies who support the library, and in any other way possible. Library trustees need not be "hidden" from the public—quite the opposite, they should be known to the community they serve. If the library has a "friends group" and it funds specific library projects, a photograph depicting the presentation of a check to the library should always include a library trustee. It is a matter of good politics to promote the library trustee in the media. It comes back to a question of mutual support between the director and the board. "The board will always want to look good, so it should be part of the librarian's political awareness to try to further that aim."[9]

It is important to promote library trustees in public relations. At the same time, it is important not to embarrass library trustees in the media. The library director must be very careful in this regard. If a trustee is to be quoted, the quotation must be cleared with the trustee in question *before* the story is released to the media. Even though the member may have said exactly what your press release states, he or she may not want it to appear in print. It is important to stress the positive contributions of library trustees in your public relations material and never ascribe blame for poor decisions. There will be times when library trustees do make poor decisions which impact the library in a less than supportive way, but these decisions can be stated for the media in a strictly factual way.

Good public relations should foster a strong working relationship between the library board and the library director. If you succeed in actively involving your trustees in positive public relations they will become interested and vocal supporters of the library in the community and will, themselves, be closely identified with library progress.[10]

THE BOARD AND THE FRIENDS GROUP

When the Friends of the Carroll Public Library was organized in 1971 it became one of only two active friends groups in the State of Iowa at that time. Strangely enough, it came into existence as a citizen reaction to a proposal by the city council to lengthen the runway at the local airport! The Library Board had been pushing for a new library building for eight years and the project had been placed on hold while more important matters were taken care of— like lengthening the runway at the airport. Support for the library in the community was suddenly galvanized and two leaders emerged to form the Friends of the Carroll Public Library. Within 18 months a bond issue for a new library building appeared on the ballot and was passed due, in large part, to the activity and organization of our friends group.

The relationship between the friends of the library and the library's board of trustees is not always a smooth one. In Carroll, a smouldering resentment of the friends group by the library board did not take long to develop. As one library trustee told me, "the friends are taking over and doing things the board ought to be doing." There was some truth in her statement, but I pointed out that members of the library board could join the friends group and participate to whatever extent they chose to do so. What I did not say was that the friends of the library were indeed "doing things the board ought to be doing," but obviously because the board was *not* doing them. The friends group developed in the first place in order to fill a vacuum. At one time our library board tried to use the friends group as a servant to perform tasks the board did not wish to undertake, but that was short-lived because the friends group rejected many of those tasks as being not in keeping with the group's purposes as outlined in their bylaws.

There are ways to help the two groups get along better, and communication between them is essential. The appointment of a liason member is one way to aid in the communication process. A member of the library board is appointed to attend all meetings of the governing body of the friends group and a member of the friends group attends all meetings of the library board. This procedure seems to work well most of the time. We have had liason members who felt uncomfortable meeting with the other group but, when this happens, a new appointment will usually take care of the problem. The president of our friends group is invited to library board meetings as an interested observer. The friends of the library needs to be careful when formulating its bylaws so that it does not intrude upon library board functions. The library director has an obligation to see that this issue is resolved to both groups' satisfaction.

The library director will need to coordinate the two groups so that they do communicate and have a cordial relationship, for both are important to the public library and its development. For many years in Carroll, the mayors refused to appoint any active or past active member of the Friends of the Carroll Library to the library's board of trustees. There was a fear that because the members of the friends group were willing to work for a better library in their spare time and fought for needed library improvements, they would soon bankrupt the city with demands for increased library funding if they became library trustees. This was a groundless argument and one which angered the Friends of the Library. At one point they confronted the mayor and demanded that a member of the Friend's board be appointed to a vacancy on the library board. Under mounting pressure, the mayor capitulated. The new trustee continued to serve on both boards and made valuable contributions to both organizations. The library's budget demands did not increase dramatically, and subsequent mayors began to appoint people to the library board who had "shown an interest in the library" by serving on the Friends' board. After three former friends of the library were serving as library trustees, the animosity between the two groups evaporated and the friends and the trustees continued to willingly serve the Carroll Library in separate capacities.

In some ways friends' groups are like advisory library boards. They wish to help the library, but have no legal responsibility to do so. They aid with fundraising activities and provide good public relations support. Because they do not govern the library, they are usually much easier to work with than the governing library board. Still many of the same techniques used with the library board work with the friends' board. Educating and informing the friends' board is just as important as with the library board. A Florida library director suggests directors "...solicit their *active* support and try to involve the board as much as possible in educating the public to the library's important services."

I am a strong believer in friends of the library groups for public libraries. They provide support from the community at large for the library and can often achieve goals or encourage library trustees to achieve goals which otherwise would be unattainable. When I look back over the accomplishments of our Friends of the Carroll Library group during the past 20 years, I wonder what we would have done without them. They saw to it that a new building was provided for the library and then moved the collections to the new location by recruiting volunteers who formed a human chain on a cold April day; they have brought nationally known speakers to our community for fundraising dinners; they raised over $2,000 one year when our book budget was inadvertently reduced by the city council; they provided over half of the match money needed for a grant application for new children's shelving and furniture; they have purchased numerous items of furniture and equipment for the library; provided us with volunteers for story hours and other jobs; promoted and publicized the library on many occasions; and made generous annual donations to the library's endowment fund. Organization of a friends of the library group can be one of the most positive public relations steps taken by any public library director.

SUMMARY

Library boards can better serve their libraries by focusing some of their talents on public relations. Working in cooperation with the library director, they bring a special perspective to this area of policy making and funding. By promoting the library to the people it serves, the board and director join in making the services, collections, and programs known to the community. The library director needs to promote the library board in dealings with the media and should see to it that the board appears in a favorable light when possible. A friends group adds another dimension to a library's public relations effort and should be encouraged to work with the board and director in a team approach.

ENDNOTES

1. James Swan, "Inside the System: A Primer for Trustees," *Wilson Library Bulletin,* 60, no. 6, February 1986: 30.

2. Guy St. Clair, and Joan Williamson, *Managing the One-Person Library.* London: Butterworth and Co., (Publishers) Ltd., 1986. p. 164.

3. Ellen Altman, ed. *Local Public Library Administration.* 2nd ed. Chicago: American Library Association, 1980. p. 48.

4. Steve Sherman, *ABC's of Library Promotion.* 2nd ed. Metuchen, NJ: Scarecrow Press Inc., 1980. p. 5.

5. Sherman, p. 4.

6. ". . .in many public libraries trustees merely play a social and ceremonial role. They rarely exercise their authority as policy-makers, they rarely flex their political muscles as library lobbyists, and they rarely put their powerful public relations potential to work for the library." Will Manly, "Facing the Public: 'Our Public Libraries are Fundamentally in the Hands of Our Trustees,'" *Wilson Library Bulletin,* 61, No. 9, May 1987: 31.

7. Rita Kohn and Krysta Tepper, *You Can Do It.* Metuchen, NJ: Scarecrow Press, 1981. p. 205.

8. St. Clair, p. 34.

9. Swan, p. 30.

10. Jean T. Kreamer, "The Library Trustee as a Library Activist" in *Public Libraries.* 29, no. 4, July/August 1990: 222.

9 LIBRARY BOARDS AND THE BUDGET

Most library boards play a critical role for the library in budget development and approval. Here again, education and communication are important factors. In order to obtain the necessary funds for the library program it is important to educate the board as to the purpose and needs of the library and persuade *them* to verbalize those needs to the governmental bodies who will supply the funding. Establishing goals with specific objectives is an essential process if increased library funding and growth are to take place.

ESTABLISHING GOALS

Budget priorities can best be developed through the exploration and approval of goals for the library, its collections, and its programs. "Planning has been defined as a rational and systematic determination of where you presently stand, where you hope to be, and how you will get to that point."[1] Many boards are reluctant to go through the time-consuming procedure of goal setting, but the development of clearly stated goals for the library should lead to a better understanding of library needs and sources of revenue. In my survey 60 percent of the library directors contacted stated that their library boards (both advisory and governing) had developed goals and objectives for their libraries. Often, when the board had not gone through this process, staff members had developed goals which the library board had then approved.

There are many pitfalls on the road to establishing the mission for the library through the goal setting process. It is possible to establish needs without setting goals, though one's chances of gaining significant increases in the library's budget are diminished if the library has no goals to aim toward. The clearer the goals and objectives are for the library, the more likely it will be that the funding can be secured to achieve them.

One of the goals adopted by the Carroll Public Library was to better publicize the library within the community. This goal was broad—as goals are meant to be—but one of its objectives—to produce a quality brochure about the library—was highly specific, as objectives should be. Both the board and the city council could understand and appreciate the need for a brochure. It led to an increase in the public relations line item in the budget and was not opposed by anyone. Preliminary research and planning gave us the approximate amount of money it would cost to produce such a brochure and that, in turn, was added to the public relations line item in the library's proposed budget. There was no problem convincing the board that a brochure was needed and that it would be necessary to increase that line item in order to cover the costs. A convinced board had no difficulty getting the increased funds from the city because it could point out this very specific need and it knew how much, almost to the penny, it would cost in terms of budget. Encourage your library board to adopt goals with objectives that are specific and attainable.

Goal-oriented boards of library trustees, in my experience, are not all that common. The goal setting process is often a long, drawn-out affair that may or may not lead to effective library improvement. Only 68 percent of the library directors who stated that their boards had developed goals agreed that the process was a positive one which resulted in measurable library improvements. Perhaps in other cases goals were not appropriate or were not supported by specific objectives.

When I began as director of the Carroll Library it was very obvious to me, as the first professional librarian in the history of the library, what needed to be accomplished. There were major deficiencies that called for an almost complete turnaround from what had been done during the first 68 years of the library's history. The board was ready for change and, in fact, had really worked hard to secure a professional in the field of librarianship. Still, the changes needed were so major and the ensuing upheaval so unnerving that it seemed that the best way to handle it was to set five-year goals for the library program.

The board was not brought into the goal setting process. I set the goals I wanted to achieve by the end of my first five years. It was very hypothetical and, in fact, I had no intention of staying as director for that long a time period, but in order to get the money needed to make immediate library improvements, very specific goals were required. I told the Board upon presentation of the "five year plan of library improvement" that I was being driven by one overpowering goal, which was to make the Carroll Library the best small library in the state of Iowa. What board could argue with a goal like that? That meeting with the board was an interesting one. Fresh out of the Library School at the University of Minnesota, I knew everything there was to know about public libraries, or thought I did. I remember telling them that the one key element in library improvement is money—that without increasing the library's budget dramatically I could do nothing.

My goal could be achieved only if the board went along with me and funded the needs I had outlined. When I had interviewed for the library director's position, the trustees had wanted to know what stood out to me as the most critical need for their library. I told them that the most glaring weakness of many weaknesses was the amount of money they were spending for books and other library materials. Later, when I accepted the position but was unable to start employment until after the new budget was adopted, they agreed to increase that line item so that I would have something to work with when I arrived. The trustees doubled the amount to be spent on library materials for me, thinking that would be more than enough, but it was still so small an amount (the line item was increased from $1,000 to $2,000) that I almost backed out and accepted a job offer at a different library!

My five-year plan called for an immediate jump in the book budget so that we could begin to replace 90 percent of the collection. I must have been very persuasive because at the very next budget meeting the board of trustees increased the book budget to $10,000 for the following year, and went as a group to the city council to get it approved (at that time the City of Carroll was our only source of income for the Library). Their selling job was based strictly on need and they offered an alternative plan— $50,000 in a one-shot deal to be spent for books. The city council looked at the disparity between the two plans and quickly approved the increase to $10,000. *Money is the critical factor in library progress.* "When adequate funds are afforded libraries, their other problems are solved easily."[2]

Another goal setting incident which comes to mind is one which involved my entire board of trustees. For many years, the Carroll Library Board studiously avoided anything that looked even remotely like goal setting. They adopted a mission statement early in my tenure and felt that was sufficient. Goals were fine as long as the library director devised them; the board was not interested in going through the tedious procedures necessary to establish goals for the library. The matter was brought up at meetings from time to time, but the consensus was: "Why should we bother setting goals when we are rapidly becoming the best small library in the state without them?" The matter came to a head when state standards for library certification dictated that "The library has a written comprehensive long-range plan covering the next three to five years which is developed by the board and staff with input from the community. . ."[3]

The board was quite torn. On the one hand it wanted certification so that everyone would know what a good library we had, but at the same time, it did not want to go through the exhaustive process of goal setting. The problem was debated at length, but finally it was decided that the board would get involved with goals and objectives through its committee structure and try to devise a long-range plan for the library. At no point during the next two years would I say that the trustees were enthusiastic about their mission! Several brainstorming sessions were held with a former trustee serving as facilitator, a community survey was made, eight goals were determined and assigned to standing committees to determine objectives, objectives were duly adopted in committee for all but one of the goals, and eventually the entire package was approved by the board, but the needed spark of enthusiasm was never present. It was something they *had* to do, not something they *wanted* to do.

As library director, I played a very minor role, partly because I wanted to see what they would come up with on their own, and partly because I was soon infected by their lack of enthusiasm. There was a collective sigh of relief when the job was more or less completed (I say more or less because they never reached objectives for one of the goals and never developed a timetable to reach any of them). The job was finished and we were able to apply for certification but, to my astonishment, the board decided at the very next meeting to disregard most of the goals they had worked on for two years and instead seek to work on six objectives which they felt *might* be achievable! Three of these objectives met needs which would require increased funding in the budget, something trustees tend to relate to easily. Obviously, they went into the goal setting task without really wanting to do so. To complicate the matter, they adopted goals which were sometimes too broad and often too vague for them to actually achieve. Further, goals they adopted looked good on paper but, even if they were all reached, they would do little in tangible terms for library improvement.

Implementation of goals falls on the library staff, a group usually already overburdened with tasks. Several library directors in my study indicated that their library boards had adopted goals for their libraries, but implementation of these goals had not occurred for a variety of reasons. Goal setting by itself will not solve the problems and move the library forward. A timetable for achieving the adopted goals must be set and implementation guaranteed. Long-range planning is vital to the success of any library program. It is an integral part of the decision-making process. Planning means that the library will be able to expand and diversify its collections and programs to meet the future as the community changes.[4]

REVENUE SOURCES GROUNDWORK

Just as library trustees need to be educated about the library, so also do the government officials who have the ultimate say in funding the library. It is very important to keep these government officials informed about the library, its collections, problems, goals, and needs. Summaries of the minutes of each library board meeting should be mailed to individual members of city councils, mayors, city managers, county governments, and any other bodies which contribute funding to the library. In Carroll, for example, the major source of revenue is the City of Carroll, but the Carroll Library also has service contracts with the local community college, the county, and seven incorporated towns within the county who either do not have their own public libraries or whose libraries cannot provide the level of service needed for their townspeople. Copies of minute summaries are sent to each town council, the dean of the college, and individual county supervisors as well as the mayor, city manager, and each person serving on the city council.

Newly elected officials should receive special mailings from the library. A few weeks before a new member is seated on the city council or county board, we send him/her a letter describing the library, its sources of funding, its service area, its goals and objectives, and its needs for continuing budget support together with a copy of the library's latest annual report and a current brochure. In this letter I congratulate the person on election to office and provide information about the library. My letter also alerts the new member to the fact that summaries of library board minutes and reports from the library will regularly be sent. Education of this type will pay off when it is time to defend the library's budget or to ask for increased funding. The education of the people who control the library's sources of funding is more challenging than that of the library board because they are further removed from the library and probably have no special interest in it.

Library trustees will probably be in personal contact with elected officials who control the library's purse strings. This is a daily fact of life in the smaller community. If they are well informed advocates of the library program, half the budget battle may already be won.

MEETING WITH THE BUDGET COMMITTEE

The committee structure of the library board is a very important one with regard to the library's budget. "Preparing a levy and a working budget may be the most critical job a library trustee will undertake during the year."[5] If you were to ask a group of randomly selected library trustees to tell you what their most important function is with regard to their libraries, a high percentage would indicate money management as the top priority.[6]

I have dealt with the library board and the library's budget both with and without a prior committee meeting. Convincing a committee and having their support in convincing the entire board is the superior way of doing it. In my early days at the Carroll Library, before the present committee structure was established, the budget meeting was always the longest meeting of the year and the budget was the only item of business on the agenda with the board acting as "a committee of the whole." Every trustee seemed to have something to say about every line item in the budget, and we often met for three hours before coming to even a tentative agreement on the library's budget. Meeting first in committee seems to smooth out the process, and we no longer need to limit the agenda for that board meeting to *just* the library's budget.

The library director prepares the initial budget proposal for the library, making recommendations for increases and/or decreases in various line items. I prefer working with this type of budget as opposed to a program budget because the more specific I am, the easier it is for all of the trustees to understand the library's needs and the easier it is for me to achieve committee support. Program budgeting, because it deals in broad programs, works for many libraries. Each library director needs to experiment with both forms to see which works best in his/her library.

In our library, the ways and means committee is charged with development of the annual budget. As library director, I present proposals for the budget in report form, justifying each increase in a line item and explaining each decrease. I write an introduction to the proposal to let the trustees know that my recommendations are merely preliminary, they serve as a starting point and the committee can modify the proposal any way it wishes before presenting it to the full board. The budget must be presented to the committee in such a way that it gives them the opportunity to make changes—that is their function in the budget process. They may not wish to do so. They may think the budget proposal you have presented is so wonderful that they need not make any changes, but they still must be given the opportunity if they so desire. A good way to do this is to include a column of blanks in the budget headed "committee recommendation" next to the column of the director's recommendations. I always include the figures for the current budget first so that it is easy to compare the year-to-year increase or decrease in each line item and in the total budget. Figure 9-1 is an example of a budget proposal for the Anytown Public Library as presented to the committee.

The budget proposal is mailed to the members of the committee several days prior to the committee meeting. This is important because you want all members of the committee to study the proposal and have a good grasp of your recommendations prior to the meeting. This is one of the times when it is a good idea to send out information to the trustees *before the meeting*. It will save time at the meeting because questions will already have been formulated by each trustee. Most of your recommended line items will pass through the committee without change, assuming that you have carefully researched your proposal and matched it to the available funding. You need to be able to justify increases in the budget to committee members. Success or failure in getting your budget proposal through the committee without a major correction will depend partly on factors you cannot control. The make-up of the committee itself will be important.

The budget process should be open to the public. For that reason, our committee usually meets over lunch in a public restaurant with notice of the meeting having appeared in the local newspaper. If a lunch meeting is not feasible for all members, we sometimes meet at 5:15 p.m. at the library. We have had budget committee meetings an hour before a scheduled meeting of the library board, but this practice tends not to work very well for us. It allows no leeway in case the discussion needs to exceed the allotted time, and often other trustees come to their meeting early and sit in on the committee meeting. Since the members of the committee are given no time to digest their final recommendation to the board, they often go into the meeting less convinced that the budget proposal is the best one they could develop and are prone to backing down at the slightest challenge by other trustees. The only advantage in this type of meeting is that the discussion is still fresh in the minds of the committee members and, for that reason, it may be easier to persuade the board to adopt the committee's wishes on the budget—especially if there is no determined opposition.

Convincing the committee to propose an adequate budget for

FIGURE 9-1   A Sample Budget Proposal

ANYTOWN PUBLIC LIBRARY

Budget Proposal: FY1993

Current Item:	Proposed Budget:	Committee Budget:	Recommendation:
Salaries, wages	$62,322	$68,398	_____
Fringe benefits	7,078	7,702	_____
Dues, memberships, etc.	600	500	_____
Training expenses	500	500	_____
Bindery	700	700	_____
Postage, freight	1,000	1,500	_____
Public relations	600	800	_____
Telephone	700	900	_____
Heat & light	12,000	12,500	_____
Supplies	5,000	5,000	_____
Furniture, fixtures	2,000	2,000	_____
Books, magazines, etc.	30,000	32,000	_____
Total:	$122,500	$132,500	_____

the library is not always easy but, once having arrived at its budget proposal, these trustees will be better able to shepherd their proposal through the library board to eventual adoption. It is important that the chair of the committee and all members of the committee have a firm grasp of the proposed budget and that they attend the board meeting where it will be discussed. To this end, the library director summarizes the committee meeting on paper and sends a copy of these minutes together with the committee's final budget proposal to each member of the committee. If there is a time lapse of more than a week between the committee meeting and the board meeting, the summary should be sent just before the board meeting as opposed to just after the committee meeting. It is too easy to forget significant parts of the budget proposal if there is a longer time lapse between meetings.

COMMITTEE BUDGET PRESENTATION TO THE BOARD

Once the committee has reached agreement on the proposed budget for the library, it becomes their task to convince the library board of trustees. The library director, having worked energetically with the committee, may or may not have succeeded in getting the kind of budget desired for the library. The committee's presentation to the board should be made by the chair of the committee, not by the library director. The library director becomes an interested party in the procedure, but should not view this presentation to the board as an opportunity to correct any errors that may have occurred in committee. The objections brought up at the committee meeting may be echoed by other trustees at the board meeting and the director may give an opinion, if asked, but should otherwise not intrude. There is always the temptation to contact other trustees before the meeting and ask them to intercede at the board meeting, but I would avoid this route. It can only lead to distrust and damage to the library program in the long run.

The library director needs to stick to the facts when dealing with the board in the budgetary process and not let emotions and desire to improve the library through increases in funding rule judgment. A library director from New Hampshire stated it this way: "I try to present information in a positive way and answer their questions straight-forwardly. I don't 'play games.'"

The full board should study the budget proposal carefully and discuss any possible changes that the trustees feel are needed. The budget at this point is still just a proposal and the board may wish to increase or decrease specific items. Individual trustees may have information about funding sources which was not available to the committee and adjustments may need to be made. The board should be unanimous in the budget they adopt for the library. Disagreements need to be worked out so that the final library budget meets everyone's approval.

My philosophy is that in nearly every instance the board will adopt a budget which is best for the library even though I may have qualms about various items. Trustees are often aware of potential funding problems that are not obvious to the library director. I can recall times when I didn't get everything I wanted in the library's budget, only to discover later that had we proposed my budget to the city council, the needed funds would not have been available to us and we might easily have provoked an across-the-board cut in our budget.

THE BUDGET DEFENSE

The defense of the library's budget to the governments who have the authority to increase or decrease the funding should fall to members of the library board. "Trustees are influential people. They can work with community leaders in ways the librarian cannot."[7] The director may or may not be a part of the budget defense. I have experienced many variations on this theme. There have been times when I, alone, presented the library's budget to the city council; times when I have presented it with the support of two or three trustees; times when the chair of the ways and means committee made the presentation with the library director attending the meeting, but not speaking; times when the chair of the committee was the only one speaking for the library; times when the entire library board and the director were present; and times when just the president of our library board was there. Library board members seem to have more success in persuading government funding bodies to increase the library's budget than do library directors.[8]

It is important to choose the best possible representative of the library for the budget presentation. This may be the library director, the board president, the chair of the ways and means committee, or someone else entirely. In critical times, when one expects the worst, it may be that you will wish to bring in support from the friends of the library or citizens from the community. It depends, of course, on the situation in which the library finds itself. There is no hard and fast rule here. The library board members are in a position to make a critical assessment of the conditions and send just one person or a delegation. There are rare times when it won't matter who goes to the meeting: either the library's budget has been rejected ahead of time and cuts will be imposed no matter what arguments are presented; or, in rare instances, the governmental body in question will be so pro-library that anything asked for by any library representative will be granted. The latter occurred for me when half the city council decided not to run for reelection and was replaced by three regular library users who then joined three others who also had active library cards. Not only did the library's budget pass without a problem (even though the requested increase was higher than that of other city departments), but I received a note of appreciation and a donation to a library project from one of the new council members the next day—and I hadn't even attended the budget presentation! Although public librarians have gone through times when their library budgets have been reduced, the majority of library directors feel that their libraries are doing quite well in funding.[9]

Some library trustees will be more powerful in presenting the library's budget demands to the funding authorities than others. We go back to the need to have powerful people on the library board. The more community power available to the board through its trustees, the more likely it is that the library's budget will have smooth sailing. There also seem to be trustees on every library board who antagonize the very people who control the finances that library needs. In most instances these board members are recognized by other library trustees and prevented from attending critical budget presentations or, if allowed to attend, are kept silent. There are times, however, when they will speak out and may sabotage the best efforts of others, but we need to keep these times to a minimum. Most library boards are able to hold these members in check.

Support for the library's budget often comes from unheralded sources. At the Carroll Library several years ago, an overzealous city manager forced the library board into a situation in which unspent funds in the library's budget and unanticipated receipts had to be "carried-over" into the city's general fund, rather than spending them for books as had always been the library board's practice. Supposedly, the board would be allowed to amend the budget and include the carry-over funds for specific projects when and if the time came. The policy was an unwritten one based only on the city manager's word with the support of the city council and mayor. Within five years, however, after the library had built up a "phantom" balance of more than $25,000—the city manager had left, the old mayor had been defeated, all six members of the city council had been replaced, and no one in city government knew anything about the library's alleged carry-over balance.

However, the story had a happy ending! One of the members of the library board's ways and means committee, who had never made a budget presentation on the library's behalf to any governmental authority, announced at the library board's budget meeting that he intended to explain the library's carry-over funds to the city council when the library's budget was defended. As library director, I provided him with the necessary background information including a direct quotation from the minutes of the library board meeting when the previous city manager had presented his carry-over funds proposal, and a year-by-year accounting of the funds the library had carried over. The board member's presentation was forceful and left no doubt in anyone's mind that the library had not only followed city procedures recommended by a city manager, but had the right to spend the money any way the library board chose and intended to use those funds in the near future to automate the library! This was another example of a library trustee who held power in the community and exercised that power in timely fashion to benefit the library.

THE BOARD AND ALTERNATE FUNDING SOURCES

The board of library trustees for any public library is also the key in providing alternate sources of funding for the library. By alternate sources, I mean not just private donations and foundation grants in aid, but all untapped sources of money for the library. When I became director of the Carroll Public Library in 1963, the Library had only one source of funding, the City of Carroll. It was a city library serving only the 6,500 citizens within its city boundaries. Anyone who lived beyond the city limits who wished to use the library could do so by paying a $1 annual fee.

That situation has changed over the years and the library now has various service contracts which supply it with funds. The population served is double that of the City of Carroll. The annual fee charged to those who are not covered by contract is the equivalent paid by city residents through their tax support of the library. Beyond that, the library participates in two programs from the State Library of Iowa which also provide funds for capital improvements and it has established its own endowment fund. In all of these sources of alternate revenue, it has been the library board working with the director which developed the needed funding. An Illinois library director wrote: "My general philosophy is to view board and administrator as a team, working together to provide the best possible service to local residents. Each provides checks and balances as well as stimulating the other party."

Not all library directors have the ability to present requests for money to public and private bodies and do so successfully. Quite often the library director is viewed as someone "with his own axe to grind," one who is seeking money to enhance his position as well as his salary. To the contrary, I believe that the vast majority of public librarians work only for the betterment of the people they serve, often to their own personal detriment. When the library director is viewed as self-seeking, however, it is of prime importance that the library's board of trustees assume a leadership role in obtaining revenue from sources other than the primary ones.

One of the goals nearly all library boards need to identify and pursue is the goal to diversify funding. *Money is the essential ingredient in positive library development.* Without it, little can be done to improve the public library's program, collections, and services. Seeking alternate sources of funding is essential and both boards of trustees and library directors need to be active in its pursuit. Special projects, bond issues for new buildings, and other capital improvements require skillful teamwork involving both the board and the director. In securing funding for these very visible library improvements, it is wise to solicit grassroots support from the friends of the library and, through them, the support of involved and concerned citizens.

SUMMARY

Goal setting and long-range planning are an important part of library development. Specific objectives can lead to increases in funding and the library director must work with his board of trustees in the budget process. Education of government authorities about the library is important and should be a continuing process. Trustees are critical players in the quest for adequate funding for our libraries.

ENDNOTES

1. Diane J. Duca, *Nonprofit Boards: A Practical Guide to Roles, Responsibilities, and Performance.* Phoenix, AZ: The Oryx Press, 1986. p. 44.

2. Daniel W. Casey, "Quality and Quantity of Public Library Service Depend on Trustees" *Public Libraries,* 24, no. 1, Spring 1985: 3.

3. State Library of Iowa, *In service to Iowa: public library measures of quality,* 2nd ed. Des Moines, IA: State Library Standards Committee, 1989. p. 8.

4. Ed Klee, "The Public Library Board is Looking for a Few Good Trustees," *Kentucky Libraries,* Winter 1989: 21.

5. John A. Lucas and Michael Madden, "A Trustee's Guide to Library Budget Building," *The Bottom Line* 3, no. 1. p. 11.

6. James Swan, "Inside the System: A Primer for Trustees," *Wilson Library Bulletin* 60, no. 6, February 1986: 28.

7. Swan, p. 30.

8. Will Manly, "Facing the Public: 'Our Public Libraries are Fundamentally in the Hands of Our Trustees,'" *Wilson Library Bulletin* 61, no. 9, May 1987: 31.

9. "In view of all the budget complaints that one hears over a period of time it is good to know that most directors are faring quite well, budgetwise. Two thirds of them get at least 90% of the money they request, 83% feel they get sufficient money to enable the library to carry on its essential services, and a good 40% are content with what they get." Robert S. Alvarez *The Library Boss: Thoughts on Library Personnel.* South San Francisco, CA: Administrator's Digest Press, 1987. pp. 173-174.

10 SALARIES, WAGES, FRINGE BENEFITS

There is a continuing concern over salaries in all types of libraries. It would seem that not a major library publication is printed without an article, letter, or statement concerning the widely recognized problem of low salaries for professional librarians. It would be an oversimplification to say that there is just one cause producing this seemingly universal problem. It is not a simple matter, but a complex one, with many causes.

A list of some of the most glaring causes of low salaries in the field of librarianship in public libraries might include the preponderance of women in the field; the availability of a large pool of qualified librarians who will accept jobs regardless of the pay; the large number of what I call "librarian pretenders" who have little or no professional training; the nature of the profession in which it is relatively easy to move on to a better paying job in another library; the absence of a professional organization with stringent requirements for membership; the failure of state libraries to set and maintain base salary minimums for qualified librarians; and the reluctance of local library boards to set a precedent by paying library directors salaries comparable to those paid to other professionals in the local community.

BOARD RESPONSIBILITIES

The determination of salaries, wages, and fringe benefits for library directors and all other library personnel is clearly the responsibility of library boards who have real power and are not just advisory in nature. The legal responsibility for salary and wage determination can be found in state law, local ordinance, and library board bylaws.

As might be expected, library boards differ in their ways of deciding wage and salary increases. Procedures may even vary with the same board of trustees from year to year. Over the years at my library, I have experienced times when the full board determined the salaries, and other times when a committee met and made recommendations to the board. Most times these recommendations have been accepted, but on occasion they have not. There have been demands made on our library board by persons who have no real say in library policy and procedures (city managers, mayors, city council people) which have been either ignored or considered depending upon the raw power contained within the library board at that time. Wages and salaries have been considered prior to the budget decision, or lump sums have been added to the budget and the division among library staff members made later in the year, usually just before the new budget takes effect. But in all of these instances and variations it has been the library board who determined the wage and salary scales, the wages and salaries offered to new employees, the cost-of-living increases granted to employees, as well as the amounts of merit increases and to whom they were awarded.

It is important for the library board to treat the director and other library employees fairly in terms of salaries, wages, and fringe benefits and, in the ideal situation, it should do so *independently* of other city, county, and district agencies. The governing library board should preserve its autonomy by placing library employees on a pay scale the board develops specifically for them, not by adopting existing pay scales of other city, county, and school units of government. If library staff salaries are below average, adoption of existing scales may result in an improvement of both wages and benefits, but it may also be detrimental to a library staff because it is very difficult to fairly equate duties and responsibilities in public libraries with those performed by other governmental workers. If the library board chooses or is pressured to go with such a plan, the determination of comparable job positions must be made by an outside, impartial "expert," not by the city manager, mayor, governmental committee, or library board.

If the library board is independent enough to be able to develop its own salary plan without outside interference, it will take into consideration salaries paid by other governmental agencies within the local community. It is a critical facet of any salary plan that it be comparable to other wages, salaries, and benefits paid locally by other tax-supported public agencies.

As director of the Carroll Public Library, it has often been pointed out to me that my salary and those of other library staff members are higher than comparable library salaries paid in similar communities in the state. My answer has always been that what is paid in other libraries in other communities should not be the determining factor in deciding what is paid to library employees in my community. There are too many variables to consider in making such a comparison. What is most important is a check of salaries paid to public employees within our own community. This is the most significant area for comparison. Exactly what is the going rate for comparable job duties and responsibilities in the local area for the population served by the library?

Salary surveys, especially to compare salaries and benefits for library directors, can be very useful, and we undertake such surveys every three to five years.[1] It is of extreme importance that the library director and staff be paid salaries and benefits that compare favorably to those earned by other city and county government employees as well as those paid to public school administrators, teachers, and clerical employees in the local community. Again, the problem will arise concerning comparable job positions. Does the library director's position equate with that of a school superintendent, principal, or other administrator, or should it be on a level comparable to a teacher? Where does the library director fall when compared to the county sheriff, the city manager, or the district engineer?

Pressure from other government officials often occurs when the library director's salary is set at a level higher than that of other city department heads. For example, the library board in Carroll was criticized by the mayor and city manager (in a private meeting) because the library director was paid a higher annual salary than that paid by the city to the police chief. Totally disregarded by city officials were the facts that the library director served a population twice the size of the city, that he had a master's degree where the police chief had a bachelor's degree, that he had more than twenty-five years' administrative experience compared to less than ten for the police chief, etc. They demanded that the library director receive no further pay raises. It is difficult for library boards, often heavily dependent upon city tax support for the library, to resist pressure of this nature.[2] The point to keep in mind, however, is that the responsibility to determine library wages, salaries, and benefits rests with the library's board of trustees and that this group must make courageous decisions for the ultimate good of the library and the community.

SEEKING BETTER SALARIES

As a graduate student at the University of Minnesota's Library School in the 1960s, my progression as a library director was outlined to me this way: I was to start my professional career at a small public library, stay there for about three years, and move on to a larger public library. I was to continue this process until, eventually, I found myself in the director's position of a large metropolitan or regional system. Each move, naturally, would involve a substantial salary boost, and I would eventually be making "good money." At that time, my professor assured me that there were 20 professional openings for every graduate of the program, so obtaining a job and moving up the ladder would not be a problem. He was right in that regard for I was offered two director's jobs even before I had obtained my master's degree, and after graduating was offered a job each time I interviewed!

What my professor didn't tell me was that staying only three years in one position is not long enough to make a significant impact on a public library nor implement the changes which are so often necessary to improve the quality of the library. If I were to stay for only three years and move on, I could never really change a public library, could never really make any lasting improvements. Being an idealist, I found this a very difficult prospect to accept. I wanted to make a lasting impact on every public library I served!

Three years is not even a long enough time to alter the thinking of members of a library board, much less make lasting improvements in a library program. I was soon asking myself "What would happen if I stayed longer?" and "Will I reach a point where my salary and benefits will attain a plateau if I *do* stay longer than the prescribed three years?"

My library board did not know what to expect in terms of my tenure. They had been somewhat spoiled by the fact that the previous librarian had stayed for 45 years! But they agreed that it had not been in the best interests of the library for her to have stayed that long. In fact, there had been so many complaints about the library in the last years of her reign that the board had literally been forced to seek someone with formal training in librarianship.

After my third year as library director I began to realize that my salary was not increasing at a very rapid clip. It seemed that I could either accept the situation, move on to a larger town, or stay and try to change library board thinking on the matter. I chose the last course and began aggressively to pursue better benefits and salary. This is a point which is often overlooked by professional librarians; one needs to be aggressive in order to gain real increases in salary and other benefits. This is not unique to our profession and partly explains the fact that teachers did not make impressive strides in salaries and benefits until they became aggressive and formed unions.

Library directors, however, can hardly be expected to unionize since they are in managerial positions and relatively isolated. But there are other ways to pursue adequate wage and salary benefits. Not only does such a stance often result in personal gains for individual librarians, there is also a "spin-off" effect which can mean gains for other library directors as well. Every time you fill out a salary survey sent to you by another library director you are helping him or her make gains if, in fact, you have been aggressive with your board and obtained reasonable gains in salaries and benefits for yourself and your staff.

A library director who does not aggressively pursue increased salary and benefits not only does a disservice to herself or himself, but to others in the profession as well. All too often, professional librarians in public libraries hold back and pretend that money is of no importance to them. They sit back and wait for their boards to recognize the superior job they are doing, hoping that this will translate into an increased salary. My experience has taught me that unless I make my salary and benefits an issue, they will be all but ignored by my library board. We have to be aggressive if we are to change an impression which has existed for many years— namely that librarianship is a service occupation where salary is not important.

It is up to each professional librarian to make the question of salary a primary concern of the board. No gains will be achieved if we sit back and expect the board to take the initiative for, in nearly all instances, this will not occur. If you are working through a committee, you must make your situation known to those committee members. If you feel you are underpaid and overworked and that your salary and benefits are inferior to those of others in your community with comparable education, training, experience, and responsibility—*it is up to you to make that fact known.* No one will do it for you. You must organize the facts and state your demands.

Being aggressive will not necessarily have positive results immediately. You may be told, as I was, that "If you don't like the salary and benefits here, you can go somewhere else." But persistence will pay off in the long run if you stick with your demands and back them up with comparisons to others within the local community and to other professional library directors in comparable communities, not just in your own state but those in states nearby. You should see solid gains in salaries and benefits for the library director and the staff. The worst thing you can do is accept the idea that your board will never change and will never offer decent salaries. You must keep after them and remember that the library board does not remain the same; each time a trustee is replaced, the balance of power shifts and a new open mind is available for input while an old, perhaps closed mind has gone off the board.

Most library boards want to know the thinking of their library director on all matters, not just those of immediate concern regarding the library. If you feel you and your staff are not receiving adequate pay or benefits, the matter must be brought to the attention of your trustees in order to change their minds and make real gains. I once pointed out to my trustees that the cost-of-living, as illustrated by the Consumer Price Index, was increasing more rapidly than my salary and, as a consequence, I was receiving the equivalent of a cut in salary each year in spite of the fact that I was moving the library forward. It was a point which my trustees had failed to notice until I brought it to their attention. Some argued that the CPI was not an appropriate measure because I was already locked into a house mortgage at a much lower percentage, but others recognized this approach as a "cop-out." The matter was referred to committee and, at the next board meeting, an automatic cost-of-living increase was adopted for all library employees, in addition to merit increases, as a library policy.[3]

FRINGE BENEFITS

Benefits will vary from library to library and even within the same library according to job classifications. It is not uncommon to see one set of benefits for professional librarians and another for nonprofessional staff members. Many employers make a distinction between full-time employees and those who work on a part-time basis. The latter are denied most benefits. My own feeling is that benefits should be awarded to all employees on a fair and equitable basis. Benefits awarded to library directors should not be different than those awarded to other library employees. To make this distinction is to invite dissension and lower productivity.

At the Carroll Library, for example, paid vacations are a benefit to all staff members except student pages (though a case could be made for applying this benefit to them as well), and are figured on an hourly basis. If a circulation clerk works thirty hours per week, she will receive thirty hours of paid vacation after one year's employment at the library. The city does not agree with the library board's policy on this matter, however. They contend that a circulation clerk who works less than forty hours per week is a part-time employee and should receive no paid vacation at all. This type of negative thinking is quite prevalent in the job market today and employers work it to their advantage by hiring many part-time employees to whom they give limited benefits, thereby reducing their out-of-hand labor costs. The fast food chains are particularly adept at this practice.

It is interesting to note that professional library directors disagree about what they consider to be benefits. A salary survey we made in 1985 rather naively asked library directors the question "What fringe benefits do you receive?" Twenty-seven different responses were received from 55 library directors with no two listing the same benefits. It was obvious that what one director considered to be a benefit, others did not. It seems likely, for example, that most everyone received paid vacation as a benefit, yet not all directors listed this as a benefit. Less than half of the directors responding to the question listed paid holidays, Social Security, and Workman's Compensation.

Library boards often grant added benefits to their library directors as a form of indirect compensation. The study referred to above uncovered a number of different benefits including the following, listed in order of the number of directors mentioning them in their answers to the question:

1. Medical insurance
2. Vacation
3. Pension
4. Sick leave
5. Life insurance
6. Holidays
7. Dental insurance
8. Social Security
9. Professional dues
10. Personal days off with pay
11. Workman's compensation
12. Expenses for meetings
13. Recreation center memberships
14. Tuition
15. Credit union
16. Other insurance
17. Paid jury duty
18. Longevity pay
19. Discount on book purchases
20. Prescription drug insurance
21. Car allowance
22. Paid funeral leave
23. Flex time
24. Paid physical examinations
25. Deferred compensation
26. Annuity plans
27. Individual retirement accounts

The list can be misleading, however, because the value of the fringe benefits varies from library to library. For example, one library director may receive medical insurance for which *part* of the premium is paid, while for someone else the library pays the entire cost. The amount of paid vacation received by library employees varies widely as well. Still, there is a variety of benefits enjoyed by public library directors as this survey illustrated.

It can be useful to inform your library board about the benefits offered in other public libraries. We go back to the process of educating the library board. Many library trustees are totally ignorant about fringe benefits, both those offered by other libraries and, surprisingly enough, those being received by library staff members in the libraries they control! At the same time, it is often easier for trustees to increase the benefits package for the library staff than to increase salaries and wages. Knowing what types of benefits are prevalent in other libraries is needed in order to make this a possibility.

GATHERING COMPARISON DATA

You should make a salary survey of other comparable libraries every three to five years. If your library is included in someone else's survey, you should be able to acquire his or her results just for having participated and that will save you a lot of time and energy. Nearly all of the surveys that come my way include a place to check to receive survey results by return mail. This is one incentive frequently offered to encourage you to return your questionnaire and thus participate in the survey. When we do a salary survey, most respondents will request a copy of the results, but I am always amazed that there will be those individuals who do not wish to receive one. Perhaps these are the library directors who are not aggressive enough in pursuing higher salaries and benefits for themselves and their employees.

You will probably benefit by doing a local salary survey annually. This type of comparison is easier to do and present to the library board. In the smaller community, the data often appears in the local newspaper. Since it is a matter of public record, however, the data is usually easy to obtain.

COMPARING WAGES AND BENEFITS AT OTHER LIBRARIES

The first thing to determine, when making a salary survey, is the data you wish to obtain. Are you going to want to know wages, salaries, and benefits for all library employees, for professional staff members only, or just for the library director? Keep in mind that the simpler the survey, the higher the rate of response. The fewer questions you can ask, the more likely it will be that your questionnaire is returned. Usually I survey just the library director's position. If I want other data, I can devise a different questionnaire. Also, many state libraries publish library staff salaries in their annual compilations of library statistics. You may be able to simplify your survey if this is true, but you will probably only be able to obtain the total amount of expenditures for fringe benefits for all library employees.

Having determined which position you wish to survey, the next step will be to devise a questionnaire which will give the data you wish to obtain. Suppose that you have decided to do a salary survey of public library directors. You must decide upon the questions you will ask. A portion of your questionnaire will include questions to verify that you are, indeed, surveying the libraries you wish to include in your final results. This is not an anonymous group of respondents here. You will need to know exactly which library pays what salary to its director, so the first question to ask is the name of the responding library and its location. It will be useful when writing up the results to be able to say that the Goodview Public Library pays its director X amount of dollars each year. This will have more clout with library trustees than to give only an average, or tell them that one unnamed library paid its director that salary.

You will need to know the population served by the library for this is an important criterion and one of the variables needed in order to make comparisons. It may also be useful to know the library's total budget and the amount spent for salaries and benefits. The items you will wish to measure are up to you and you will want to include questions which, when applied to your library, will show you in the best possible light. For example, when preparing the questionnaire for my first library directors' salary survey I included questions concerning total budget and amounts spent by the library each year for salaries and benefits because I knew our library would rank toward the bottom on both measures. The other variables you may wish to include are the library director's education, the number of years experience as a director, the number of years employed at the present library, the fringe benefits received, and the annual salary. Try to keep the survey as short as possible while still obtaining the necessary comparison data.

The next step will be to determine which libraries to survey. Devise a list of libraries which are comparable to your own library statistically. If you just survey a random list of libraries, your results will be of limited value. The initial survey will determine the group of comparable libraries in your survey. Surveys sent in succeeding years will use the same basic list of libraries with modifications. For example, the first survey my staff and I did went to public libraries serving populations between 10,000 and 50,000. We wanted to compare our library to others in towns large enough so that the library director could be expected to have a degree in library science. We also wanted the libraries to have budgets of less than $500,000 and to be individual public libraries, not systems. The survey was to include public libraries in Iowa and some of the nearby states. In determining the group of public libraries to be surveyed we used the *American Library Directory* and compiled a list of every public library which met these criteria. The list included 72 public libraries. Even with careful selection, we received responses from libraries which did not meet our criteria. In some, the population served was larger than that indicated in the *American Library Directory* and in others the budget exceeded our limit. One library in our survey was headquarters to a large system. In subsequent surveys these libraries were deleted from the group.

Library directors respond well to salary surveys. From our group of 72 in 1985 we received 54 responses within the time limit specified and five additional responses after that time had expired. We found that several libraries failed to respond because the library director's position was vacant at the time we sent our survey. A cover letter explaining the reasons for the survey and encouraging participation is important. The letter can be personalized using the computer or it may be sent using a generic form of address like "Dear Library Director." Using your library stationery, the cover letter may look like the example in Figure 10-2. The questionnaire, cover sheet, and return envelope are then mailed to each library director in the survey population. Because the libraries have been selected from a publication which is probably somewhat out-of-date and the fact that library directors do switch jobs fairly often, it is better to address the envelopes to the library director rather than to a specific person.

Tabulation of the responses and writing the analysis are fairly easy using a computer. As the returns come in, they are tabulated on various templates depending on which variables you wish to

FIGURE 10-1   A Salary Survey Form

SALARY SURVEY

Name of Library _____

Location _____

_____

Population served (include areas served by contract) _____

Library Director's education (highest degree attained) _____

Total library budget _____

Total library budget for salaries & fringe benefits _____

Number of years experience as a library director _____

Number of years at current library as director _____

Library director's annual salary _____

Continued

FIGURE 10-1 *Continued*

Check the fringe benefits you have:

medical insurance_____   dental insurance_____   prescription drug plan_____

Social Security_____   pension_____   life insurance_____

professional dues_____   car allowance_____   paid vacation_____

workman's compensation_____   paid sick leave_____   paid holidays_____

meeting expenses_____   tuition_____   paid personal days_____

paid funeral leave_____   paid jury duty_____   credit union_____

longevity pay_____   flex time_____   paid physical exams_____

deferred compensation_____   annuity plan_____   book purchase discount_____

IRA_____   other (please specify)_____

_____

Do you wish to receive a copy of the results of this survey?   Yes   No

Please return this form to **Gordon Wade, Carroll Public Library, 118 East 5th St., Carroll, IA 51401** by December 15, 1991. Thank you! [4]

FIGURE 10-2   Example of a Cover Letter

November 12, 1991

Dear Library Director:

We are making a survey of library directors' salaries in the Midwest
and hope that you will help us by filling out the enclosed one-page
questionnaire. We are seeking to compare educational achievement,
experience, population served, fringe benefits, and salaries for
library directors in a six state area including Iowa, Minnesota,
Illinois, North Dakota, South Dakota, and Nebraska. Please use data
for the current operating year.

A stamped self-addressed envelope is enclosed for your convenience
and we will be happy to send you a copy of the results of our survey
if you wish to receive one. We have set a cut-off date of December
15, 1991 and we would appreciate having your response back by that
date. Thank you for helping us!

Sincerely,

Gordon Wade
Library Director

compare. You may wish to exclude responses if they don't meet your original criteria for inclusion in the study. Occasionally you will receive a usable response from a library director who does not want the name of his library used. When this happens, you can list the library under a pseudonym like "Library A." The raw data is listed alphabetically by the name of the town in which the library is located, as shown in Figure 10-3.

You may also wish to include all the other variables from the questionnaire, and computer programs are available which will allow you to do this. When another questionnaire is returned, the data can be inserted in alphabetical order. In this way the data from each questionnaire is added until your predetermined cut-off date is reached. This is just raw data, however. It doesn't tell you or your library board a whole lot until it has been changed into a series of rankings. Note that the fringe benefits column consists of numbers which represent the various fringe benefits on our questionnaire. Note also that the name of your library always appears in capital letters wherever it appears in the tabulations. This serves to draw the attention of our trustees to our position in the rankings.

The first ranking you will want to do is to rank all the libraries by the director's salary starting with the highest salary first. An abbreviated list would look like Figure 10-4. You will probably have at least 50 libraries in your ranking and *your* salary will probably not be the highest one of those directors surveyed. This ranking shows your library board members how your salary compares to that of other library directors in similar communities in a specified geographical area. The lower you are in the ranking, the better your chances are of getting salary improvement. Keep in mind, however, that there are other variables to consider. Some of these variables will have been measured by the questionnaires and will show up in other rankings, but some, like the quality of library service you are providing to your community, will not.

There are several interesting things you can do with a ranking. You can figure out the average salary and compare that to your salary; you can divide the ranking into thirds and see where you stand; you can look at the top ten salaries or the bottom ten salaries and draw a comparison with your salary. The comparisons you wish to emphasize will depend, in part, on where your salary falls in the ranking. You might find yourself at a great advantage to be at the bottom of the list or to have a disadvantage to be near the top. In 1985 when I did my first survey, my salary was above average, but not in the top ten. My salary ranked 19th out of 54.

FIGURE 10-3   Tabulation of Survey Responses

Library:	Director's salary:	Education:	Experience:	Fringe benefits:
Abraham, IL	$32,500	M.L.S.	26	1,3,4,7,9,11
Beauty, KS	21,000	B.L.S.	18	1,2,5,8
CARROLL, IA	28,000	M.L.S.	22	1,2,3,4,5
Fairview, IA	18,500	M.L.S.	3	1,2,6,9,23
Goody, SD	23,900	M.L.S.	7	1,2,8,10,22
Heaven, MN	29,300	M.L.S., M.P.A.	9	1,3,5,10,21
Zither, NE	25,000	B.L.S.	12	1,2,7,17,18
Library A	29,000	M.L.S.	14	1,2,3,4,5,11

Being above the midpoint of 27 was a disadvantage, but I countered that by pointing out that the top salary in the ranking was nearly $11,000 a year higher than mine while I was earning less than $9,000 more than the person at the bottom! My library board was reassured because they were paying me above the average salary in the survey but, at the same time, they could see that there was room for improvement.

The next ranking I did was by years of experience and salary. I went back to my raw data tabulation and pulled out those two variables and ranked the 54 libraries in terms of the library directors' years of experience. With 22 years as director of the Carroll Public Library, I ranked fifth from the top. I had hoped to show that the more years of experience a library director had, the higher his salary, but the results of the survey didn't turn out that way. In my comparison directors with 10 to 14 years experience earned more on average than did directors with 20 to 24 years

```
FIGURE 10-4   Ranking Salaries


      Library:                    Director's Salary:

      Abraham, IL                      $32,500
      Heaven, MN                        29,300
      Library A                         29,000
      CARROLL, IA                       28,000
      Zither, NE                        25,000
      Goody, SD                         23,900
      Beauty, KS                        21,000
      Fairview, IA                      18,500
```

experience.[5] It is important to include data in the survey even though it does not work to your advantage, for this builds an element of honesty into the survey results and analysis and shows your library board that you are not attempting to bend the data or exclude contrary data to benefit your own point of view. I broke this ranking down into five-year increments and computed an average for each group. Even though the 10 to 14 years experience group earned more than the 15 to 19 and the 20 to 24 year groups, it was valuable to include it in the study because the average salary earned by those with less than eleven years experience was significantly lower than the other three groups.

Next I did a rank order of libraries by population served and director's salary. Again, this did not prove to be to my advantage for my salary was above average for the group of libraries serving a population between 15,000 and 25,000, but here again I was able to point out that the top salary in my population group was considerably higher than mine and that there were seven library directors serving a similar population to Carroll's who were earning more than I earned. You have your choice of points to emphasize in each ranking. There will be negatives as well as positives, but you can choose to elaborate on the positive features of the ranking and ignore the negatives (although they are there for your trustees to comment about, if they wish).

Rankings can then be made for all of the other variables included in the survey except fringe benefits. A ranking of total budgets in my 1985 survey showed that only six other libraries had smaller total budgets than the Carroll Library and only three other libraries spent less on salaries and benefits. While this information was not particularly useful in getting *my* salary increased, it did have a positive effect on future budgeting. My trustees frequently referred back to this point when discussing the library's budget increases and I reminded them of it as well.

The fringe benefits awarded library directors at other libraries can be listed in a rank order starting with the most benefits checked. Remember that this survey is merely to find out what benefits are offered by other public libraries. You are not trying to compare benefits on a basis of quality, merely quantity. You could do a survey just on benefits if you needed to know their precise values and how your library compares.

Rankings are fine, but they need to be interpreted and analyzed for the library board. Again, it is best to keep it simple. Salary surveys provide great quantities of data and the temptation will be to interpret too much of it for the library board. It is better to resist this temptation and condense it down to the bare essentials. The longer your analysis is, the less likely it is that your trustees will wade through it all. Five or six double-spaced pages should be ample to draw your board's attention to the results of the survey and make the significant points needed to improve your own salary and benefits.

An introductory paragraph tells the reason the survey was made and the criteria used in selecting the libraries included in the survey. A couple of paragraphs are used to describe the survey: when it was sent out, how many were sent, how many were returned, the cut-off date, how the data was tabulated, etc. Any complications occurring which may have limited the usefulness of the data need to be stated. This is followed by a description of the rankings and any tables which may have been compiled. The remaining pages of the analysis portion should be used for making the comparisons between your library and the others surveyed and drawing any conclusions you may wish to make. It is a good idea to provide a cover for the report as well as copies of the cover letter and the questionnaire itself, a list of the libraries who did respond and a list of those who did not, and the rankings and tables of data to which readers of the report may wish to refer.

Assemble your report just as you would other library reports written to educate and enlighten your board of trustees. Use of a computer-generated cover (without a picture), various colors of paper, and thoughtful layout will greatly enhance the effectiveness of the report. A carefully designed, well-written salary survey will provide dividends both for you and your board.

COMPARING WAGES AND BENEFITS OF LOCAL PROFESSIONALS

As we have learned, one of the difficulties in salary comparisons is determining the job categories comparable to that of a professional library director or other library staff member. The smaller the population served, the more difficult it is to find a pool of other professionals with which to compare one's position. My board has indicated to me that they do not wish to compare my duties, responsibilities, education, experience, and salary with occupations in private industry, but that they *do* see a point of comparison between my salary and benefits and those of other professionals who are being paid money raised through property taxes. This limits the comparison group, in my case at least, to employees of the city, the county, regional government agencies, and the public school system.

Your first step in making a local salary and benefits comparison will be to decide which positions in your community will make up the comparison pool. The library board should discuss comparable job positions and give you their ideas as to which occupations they feel are comparable. My board, for example, agrees that my salary should be comparable to those paid to public school principals and other administrators and so we will include these positions in our survey rather than teachers. We also want to look at salaries and benefits paid to city department heads, elected county officials, and heads of regional government agencies. Comparable positions available for use in comparison studies will vary from state to state and from community to community. Each library director will have to confer with his or her board of trustees in order to determine the make-up of a local comparison pool.

Getting the data should not be a problem since salaries and benefits paid in local and regional governments are generally a matter of public information. Furthermore, sharing the results of the survey will usually benefit everyone covered by the survey, which promotes a degree of participation. You need to obtain information concerning educational levels, years of experience, benefits received, and salaries for each position surveyed. Another important piece of information to learn is the population served by the position. County officials will sometimes serve a larger population than city and/or school officials. The library director may serve a population which includes all of the areas served by other positions in the survey, and could include others as well. It is important to know what populations are served. It can be a convincing factor to point out, for example, that the library director is called upon to serve both the city and county populations while the police chief deals only with the population found within the city limits. You need to individualize your questionnaire so that it will provide the information you feel is important to know when comparing your salary and benefits to those of others in your community.

The survey needs to be kept simple and it is wise to offer to share the data with each participant after the survey is completed and the results written up. A cover letter is needed and the forms may be mailed to the individuals in the comparison pool. You may need to follow up with a telephone call if a response is not received before the cut-off date. In difficult instances, where the individual does not wish to provide the data you need, you may have to contact the controlling board or higher official. I have found that individuals in local and regional government are usually very cooperative in providing salary and benefit data when the purpose of the survey is stated.

Just as with the comparative salary survey of library directors, when asking for information on benefits it is best to list the benefits and ask the recipient to check a list rather than asking an open-ended question like "What benefits to you have with your job?" You should always leave blanks for a category labled "other" just in case your list does not include all of the benefits a job provides.

Your cover letter and survey form should be mailed to each participant you have selected for your comparison with a stamped, addressed return envelope. The actual form of the questionnaire will be very similar to the form sent to other librarians and will yield interesting data for comparison purposes. Each questionnaire can be personalized by position rather than asking that specific question. The questionnaire sent to the city police chief might look like Figure 10-5.

When doing a survey of this type, you may not need to send individual surveys to each participant. The city manager or comparable official could provide you with all the data you need for each city department head, the school superintendent for each school administrator, etc. Sending the questionnaires to one person in

FIGURE 10-5   Survey Form for Local Professionals

SALARY SURVEY

Position: *City Police Chief*

Location: *Carroll, Iowa*

Population served: _____

Police chief's education (highest degree attained): _____

Number of years experience as a police chief: _____

Police Chief's annual salary: _____

Check the fringe benefits you have:

medical insurance_____	dental insurance_____	prescription drug plan_____
Social Security_____	pension_____	life insurance_____
professional dues_____	car allowance_____	paid vacation_____
workman's compensation_____	paid sick leave_____	paid holidays_____
meeting expenses_____	tuition_____	paid personal days_____
paid funeral leave_____	paid jury duty_____	credit union_____
longevity pay_____	flex time_____	paid physical exams_____
annuity plan_____	deferred compensation_____	

other (please specify)_____

_____

Do you wish to receive a copy of the results of this survey?   Yes   No

Please return this form to **Gordon Wade, Carroll Public Library, 118 East 5th St., Carroll, IA 51401** by December 15, 1991. Thank you!

authority rather than to individuals is easier and will often provide more complete participation. People may be reluctant to fill out survey questionaires on an individual basis. Benefits will probably be the same for all positions in each governmental agency, further simplifying the process.

When all of the questionnaires have been returned, you simply list them in one ranking from the highest salary to the lowest with separate columns for education and experience. In the body of your report you will note discrepancies in population served and fringe benefits received. Your tabulation might look like Figure 10-6.

Just seeing this ranking by itself would have considerable impact in influencing a library board. The focus should be on where the library director's salary falls in comparison to the others in the survey. There are many angles from which one can view the data and produce convincing arguments. Since library directors tend to be underpaid, it is easy to point this out in such a ranking. In this example, the library director is the lowest paid position for persons with master's degrees or better (figuring that the county attorney would be making $44,000 were he employed on a full-time basis). The library director also has the highest number of years of job experience of anyone in the survey. His salary is 12th from the top out of 19 positions surveyed. The body of the report will include these observations along with any statistical notations that need to be made (the average salary is $35,700 if we figure the county attorney at his full-time equivalent, for example, placing the library director $5,700 below average).

A comparison of job benefits also needs to be made. A table at the back of the report will list all of the benefits checked by persons completing the survey and will also list the library director's benefits as a point of comparison.[6]

Your library board may ask you to compare your salary and benefits with those earned by teachers in the local public school. Even though the jobs are not comparable, it will probably be to your advantage to cooperate and make the comparison. Keep in mind, however, that your job covers the full year, while teachers usually work a nine-month year. This factor needs to be taken into consideration by figuring and comparing monthly salaries as opposed to annual salaries. Suppose a teacher with the same amount of education and experience as you have as library director earns $28,000 per year. Your $30,000 per year would make you appear to earn more, but on a monthly basis you would be making less. (If you received one month of vacation you would divide your salary by eleven and the teacher's salary by nine giving you a

FIGURE 10-6   Compiling a Table of Local Salaries

LOCAL COMMUNITY SALARY SURVEY

Position:	Salary:	Education:	Experience:
School superintendent	$55,000	PhD Ed.	15 years
High school principal	46,000	M.S. Ed.	21 years
City manager	41,500	M.P.A.	6 years
Grade school principal	41,000	M.S. Ed	13 years
Middle school principal	39,800	M.A.	11 years
County Engineer	39,700	B.S.	4 years
School business manager	38,000	M.S. Ed.	9 years
Regional govt. director	35,000	B.A.	2 years
City engineer	34,900	M.S.	6 years
County sheriff	33,100	A.A.	24 years
City clerk	28,500	High school	20 years
LIBRARY DIRECTOR	28,000	M.A.	25 years
City police chief	27,500	B.S.	8 years
Parks & recreation head	27,400	B.A.	11 years
County treasurer	26,000	High school	21 years
Ambulance director	25,800	B.A.	15 years
County auditor	25,750	B.A.	4 years
Clerk of Court	25,750	High school	11 years
County attorney (half-time)	22,000	Juris D	6 years

monthly salary of $2,727.27 and the teacher $3,111.11.) You also need to underline the fact that teachers may use their three months of vacation in the summer to further educate themselves. The hours they spend often result in an advancement on their pay scale, a benefit most library directors do not enjoy.

WRITING THE REPORT

Salary comparison reports are written up just like all other library reports to the board. Keep in mind that one of the purposes of the report is to educate the library board about library salaries and how they compare with salaries and benefits of other librarians in similar communities and other tax-paid professional people in the local community. Your ultimate goal is to increase the salaries paid in your library. This is not to say that you should suppress facts which do not support favorable board action on this matter. Attempts to do so will be perceived by your trustees as a subterfuge and may negate gains you would have made had you included all the facts. For example, the salary survey I made in 1985 showed that my salary and benefits were below average when compared to other library directors in a five state area, but above average when compared to other library directors in Iowa. Rather than ignore the latter and risk having it pointed out by a trustee, I incorporated it into my report. Several library trustees were surprised that I included it, but by doing so I added a degree of integrity and fairness to my report which gave the board the feeling that the report was not necessarily slanted in my favor. By incorporating *all* of the facts into the report one defeats much of the opposition before it is generated, and the impact of negative data is reduced.

You may want to include information other than that gleaned by your surveys. It may be useful to use the annual salary data published in the *Library Journal*. How does your salary compare to that of recent library school graduates? You usually summarize the appropriate data from this source in your report using just one paragraph. You can make a revealing and very persuasive graph by comparing your salary with the annual increase in the cost-of-living. The difference between your annual salary adjusted for inflation compared to your actual annual salary is often miniscule. I once made this comparison over a twenty-year period and found that my actual take home pay adjusted for inflation had increased less than $500 per year. It was a real "eye-opener" for my trustees who felt they had provided me with ample merit increases over the years until they saw that graph.

Your report should also include recommendations, even though they probably will be for an increase in *your* salary and benefits. Too often we, as professional librarians, shy away from this procedure, thinking that if we present the data our library trustees will make the proper connection and raise our salaries and benefits. Some boards will take the lead and follow through with a significant increase, but other boards (and I think perhaps the majority of trustees) will see the lack of specific recommendations as a way of bailing out. I would rather make a specific proposal that my salary and benefits be increased by a certain amount and have my board turn it down than risk losing the initiative by not making my wishes known to them. Better to have fought and lost than not to have fought at all! It goes back to my belief that librarians are not aggressive enough when it comes to their own salaries and benefits. It's too easy to wait for one's trustees to recognize what seems to us to be an obvious situation, rather than to go on the offensive and actively pursue a better salary.

CONVINCING THE COMMITTEE

If your library board is operating under a system of committees, there will be one charged with making salary and benefit recommendations to the full board so your first job, having gathered the data and written a convincing report, will be to present it to the committee and get them on your side. Because of the complexity of salary and benefit comparison survey reports, it will be necessary for committee members to read the report before the committee meeting. There are risks involved in this procedure. Some members may get together privately before the meeting and discuss the report even though such a clandestine meeting is unethical and even illegal where there are open meetings laws. When this does occur, it may not involve all committee members and this will cause hard feelings among those not included. It may seem the matter has been decided before the committee gets together. Still, the report will contain so many facts and comparisons that prior perusal of the data is a necessity if the committee is to come to a conclusion and be able to make a united recommendation to the full board.

In my opinion, when such a report is not delivered to members before the committee meets, there is a tendency to table the matter and call for a second meeting after the report can be carefully scrutinized by committee members. When this happens, one realizes that the report might as well have been distributed prior to the meeting. I think we have to assume that there will be discussion of the report among committee members prior to the meeting but, if the report is strong enough and makes recommendations based on the facts gained through the surveys, these visits between committee members may have no effect on the outcome.

Convincing the committee to make useful recommendations to the board is vital to the success of a salary proposal. When a recommendation or set of recommendations is reached by the committee it needs to be written up and distributed to all members of the committee. It is neccessary to write the minutes of the committee meeting and send a copy to each member so that they know the content of the recommendations to be presented to the library board on this matter. The committee chair will refer to these minutes when making the presentation.

COMMITTEE PRESENTATION TO THE BOARD

A united committee will make a more convincing presentation of the facts and salary recommendations to the board than will a divided committee. It may be that the chair of the committee wishes to delegate making the proposal to another committee member who is, perhaps, more persuasive. Copies of the salary survey report will need to be available for other members of the board at the meeting should they need more information about the committee's recommendations.

The library director is an interested observer in this matter when it is presented to the board. Although the best-informed person on the facts at this time (having created the questionnaires, compiled the data, written the report, and convinced the committee), the director needs to take a "back-seat" to the committee spokesperson, ready to provide technical assistance, but not attempting to persuade the board to adopt the committee's recommendations or reject them. The library director has already influenced the committee as much as possible to arrive at equitable solutions to a problem with strong personal overtones. Let the committee do the persuasion.

Just as in any other library board meeting, things can go wrong. If it is possible within the framework of your agenda, it will be better to schedule the salary proposal toward the end of the meeting. Even though it is a committee report and would normally fall near the beginning of the meeting, I try to place salary recommendations in the latter part of the agenda under new business. This will give trustees the chance to "warm up" to each other through the discussion of other items of business, and they will have had the opportunity to reject several proposals which will clear the way for favorable adoption of the salary proposals. I am always a little leery if the board reaches the salary recommendation item without having turned down at least one proposal. The psychology of not wishing to rubber stamp the library director comes into play and the salary proposal fails not because of inherent weakness in the recommendation, but merely because the board does not wish to agree with the library director on everything.

DEFENDING LIBRARY SALARIES

Assuming that the salary surveys, report, and committee recommendations have been successful and the library board has approved increases in library salaries and benefits, what happens when other government officials decide to challenge them? Whether or not this situation develops will depend on the degree of autonomy and power held by the library board. If the board is weak and has a tradition of following city and county practices, it may easily find itself being criticized by government officials if library salaries and wage scales exceed those paid by other government agencies, or if individual salaries and benefits increase at a higher rate.

Once the salary recommendation has been passed by the library board, the matter is really out of the library director's hands. The responsibility for defending salaries and benefits rests with the library board. They, of course, can cite the information contained in the report which includes the salary surveys. The information which convinced the library board to increase salaries and benefits can then be used to convince government officials of the correctness of their action. Don't allow yourself to be forced into defending your own salary and benefits—once the action is taken by your board it is their problem, not yours!

As my salary and benefits have risen, so has the pressure put on my library board by the mayor and city manager. My library board has successfully defended their action each year because they were armed with factual information which was indisputable. On occasion, city officials have countered by presenting their own salary surveys of library directors in other towns, but these surveys have been successfully challenged by library trustees because they rarely take into consideration factors of comparable populations, director experience and qualifications, and quality of library service. In no instance have I entered the fray—it is really no longer my concern once it has been approved by my board. It is their responsibility to procure the necessary funds.

SUMMARY

Librarians must be aggressive if they are to achieve and maintain salary levels comparable to others with similar education, experience, and responsibility. Surveys of salaries and benefits paid to other library directors as well as other comparable professional employees of government agencies within our communities will be helpful in convincing our library boards to pay us the salaries and benefits we deserve.

ENDNOTES

1. When doing a salary survey keep in mind that you will be able to measure quantitative variables, but not qualitative ones and *both* are important. You may, for example, be able to compare your library's salaries and fringe benefits to those of other libraries serving similar populations with budgets close to yours with approximately equal collection sizes—libraries which are similar to your library in many ways statistically—but you won't be able to measure the quality of library service being offered in each community and be able to say which library is best at serving its users. This is important, because library directors and other staff members who are performing their duties in an outstanding manner deserve to be paid more than their counterparts in other communities who may be doing only an average job.

2. To my board's credit, the president relayed the board's message to the mayor and city manager that they didn't really care what salary was paid to the police chief. If the city council felt he was not being paid enough, they should raise his salary. It was not a concern of the library board if the police chief earned more than the library director.

3. I must confess that this provision did not last for long. Eventually, in the face of double digit gains in the Consumer Price Index, the policy was rescinded. While it was in effect, however, library salaries more than kept up with the cost-of-living. Later, after increases in the rate of inflation declined, the practice was reinstated.

4. It is very important to include your name and address on the questionnaire even though you will probably include a self-addressed, stamped envelope to help insure its return. Questionnaires and envelopes are frequently separated and when the time comes to return the survey, the recipient will have no idea where to send it unless the return address has been made a part of the questionnaire. A cut-off date is also important. Without a specific date to aim for many responses will be received long after they can be included in the results.

5. Library directors with 10 to 14 years experience earned an average of $30,608.55 compared to $29,704.00 earned by those with 20 to 24 years experience.

6. It always surprises me when I learn that no trustee on my library board seems to know what benefits I receive even though that information comes up frequently when we discuss salary and benefit improvements!

11 COMPARISONS WITH OTHER LIBRARIES

The director of a library strives to make his or her library the best it can possibly be. That should be the goal, but is one which is probably never attained because the conditions keep changing. Progress will be made and should be related to the board of trustees. Making a statistical comparison of the library to those in similar communities will provide a yardstick on which to measure library progress and will be enlightening to trustee and director alike.

WHY COMPARE?

Drawing a comparison between your library and other libraries is a very effective tool for initiating needed library change and improvement. It doesn't matter where your library falls in the comparison, whether you are the best, the worst, or somewhere in between. Your position, when compared to peer libraries, can be used with the board of trustees to improve the adequacy of your library. Educating your board is the answer. Library boards will not be able to measure how well the library is operating unless they have some way of gauging the library's performance.[1]

Individually and as a group, trustees are curious to know how their library compares to the one serving a similar population down the road. A statistical comparison using data often available from your state library or obtained by sending out a questionnaire or survey will provide the answers. Keep in mind that no library trustee wants an "average" library. Only in comparison with other libraries can one know whether or not the library one serves is fulfilling its commitment to excellence. A library director from Ohio explained: "Trustees want to be a part of a noteworthy institution. The library's success will be reflected onto the trustees. Once the process begins, the director/board relationship will build rapidly."

CHOOSING LIBRARIES TO COMPARE

Population should be the determining factor in deciding the group of 6 to 15 libraries in your comparison base. You will need to

161

determine the populations served by these other libraries and decide how much of a variation from your population to include in the comparison. Obviously, you may not be able to find 6 to 15 other public libraries in your state which serve populations exactly the same as yours. However, it is a good idea to compare your library to other libraries serving populations which do not vary more than 20 percent either way from your library's primary population or service area. Say your primary population is 10,000 people. To stay within the 20 percent guideline you would be comparing your library to all other public libraries in your state serving primary populations between 8,000 and 12,000. If you exceed the 20 percent variation, the validity of your study may be challenged.

You will also need to discover what the population listed for the other libraries includes. Do your population figures relate to "population served" or do they refer merely to the primary population of the city or town in which your library is located? The Carroll Library, for example, is located in a town of 10,000 people and that is its primary population. But the library has contracts which, together, increase the service area for the Library to 18,500 people. Should the Carroll Library compare itself to other towns of 10,000 or to other libraries serving 18,500 people? The statistics published by the State Library of Iowa ignore population served and list statistics by primary population so we are forced to compare on a primary population basis. To be absolutely accurate we would need to go through the time-consuming process of compiling our own statistics, but even then librarians are not always knowledgeable in making a distinction between "primary population" and "population served."

The larger the population of your community, the more difficult it will be for you to find other libraries your size in your state with which you can compare. Larger libraries may have to cross state lines in order to find a group of similar libraries within population guidelines. Fortunately, the collection of public library statistics is based on uniform definitions, so comparisons should have validity when comparing to similar libraries in other states.[2] If you wanted to, of course, you could prepare a survey questionnaire and mail it to libraries selected by primary populations rather than depending upon published statistics, but this would be very time-consuming and probably unnecessary. If the statistics have already been gathered for you and they are reliable, you should take advantage of them.

When deciding upon the make-up of libraries in your comparison group you may also wish to include a couple of libraries which are outside your chosen parameters. You might include a larger library, for example, which has a reputation for mediocrity, and a smaller library which exceeds everyone's expectations. Examples of libraries of these types are fairly easy to find and are useful in comparisons because of their variance from the expected norm.

GATHERING THE DATA

Suppose, then, that you have determined, by primary population served, that there are six other public libraries in your state with which you can compare your library, and you have found one larger library which has the reputation of being below average and one smaller library which is statistically superior. Now you need to gather comparative data. You will need to make a table by populations of the libraries you hope to include in your comparison. The Anytown librarian's comparison base looked like Figure 11-1.

Note that Northland is more than 20 percent larger than Anytown and Pleasantridge is more than 20 percent smaller. These variations will need to be noted when the study is completed and ready for presentation.

Your first choice in obtaining the data necessary to draw your comparisons is to have someone else gather it for you! State libraries are great sources of information for comparing public libraries and you should use them if at all possible. Annual compilations of comparative data are frequently distributed by state libraries and may already be available to you. Use the most current data published. You may wish to check with your state library to find out when the newest compilation will be available and plan your comparisons for a time soon after its publication.

If your state library does not provide library statistics, you will need to request the information directly from the libraries in your selected group. A one page questionnaire should provide you with the statistical data you need. Most librarians will cooperate by sending you detailed information about their libraries if you request it using a brief survey form along with a cover letter telling them why you are making the comparison and offering to share the results. When tabulating the answers to your questions, it is important to make sure that the statistics are truly comparable. A sharp variation on one library's return may indicate a misunder-

FIGURE 11-1   Comparing Towns

Town:	Population:
Northland	15,037
Fairpark	11,987
Green Meadow	11,255
Iron City	10,766
Landview	10,410
ANYTOWN	10,000
Mountaintop	9,381
Hilltown	8,147
Pleasantridge	5,421

standing of the question, and a follow-up telephone call may be needed to clarify the matter. Compilations of statistics by state libraries are not immune to error either. You need to check with the library director of a given library when a noticeable deviation occurs.

DECIDING WHICH DATA TO USE

If you are able to use statistics from your state library you will probably find that they will provide you with more comparative measures than you can possibly use. The 1988-1989 issue of *Iowa Public Library Statistics,* for example, provides detailed statistics for 64 different measures of public library adequacy.[3] To make a comparison between your library and the other libraries in your study on every measure available to you would be mind-boggling, to say the least. Your purpose in making the comparisons is to educate your library trustees, not confuse them; you must be selective in the data you choose to present.

You need to determine which measures are the most important ones and are items that are easily compared and easily grasped by lay people. But you also need to keep in mind what it is you hope to improve about your library. If you feel that your materials budget is too low, you will want to compare that measure of adequacy with those of your peer libraries, but you may also wish to use other indirect measures of materials budgets like, for example, the number of volumes added each year. In the same way, if you feel that your library's main problem is a lack of space, you might wish to include measures which will highlight this difficulty, like square feet of building space and/or linear feet of shelving. To make your comparisons meaningful, you must choose measures of adequacy for which your trustees will have ready applications in your library and these will vary from library to library. You need to determine which of the statistics available to you will best illustrate the weaknesses and strengths of your library. The measures you choose will be dependent upon the way you wish to show your library.

It is wise to include some data which make your library look good if for no other reason than to positively reinforce your library board for improvements they *have* authorized. Suppose, for example, that you have adequate space for your library's collections, but you feel that your library needs more money to purchase new videocassettes. Comparative data on video expenditures show your library to be near the bottom when compared to others serving similar populations. You will definitely want to include a table of video expenditure comparisons, but you might also wish to include a building square foot table which shows your library to be superior to many of the others. This is a way of achieving balance and showing your board that your library has made progress in some areas. This reinforces their belief in themselves as a functioning board and encourages them to make even more improvements.

In order to decide which rankings to include in your comparison survey, you need to first determine the strengths and weaknesses of your library. As librarians, we all should know which areas of our libraries are adequate and which are substandard. If, perchance, you do not know your library's weak and strong points, the statistical comparisons you make will certainly highlight them. In order to improve, you will need to underline the library's weaknesses for the library board. It is helpful to list the library's strengths and weaknesses as you perceive them *before* you look at the statistics. The Anytown librarian listed the following strong and weak points for that library:

Strengths:
Appropriations
Building size
Materials budget
Size of collections
Circulation

Weaknesses:
Video expenditures
Number of magazine subscriptions
Salaries and wages
Number of staff members
Fringe benefits

From this list she knew which comparisons she wanted to make for her library board both to underline the strong points and pinpoint weak areas of the Anytown Public Library.

When you compare your library to others you will need to group your rankings together by content. All measures of collection strength are placed close to one another in the study, as are matters of appropriations and other measures which have a relationship. Tables for staff size, salaries, and fringe benefits should appear near each other since they are related. There will be some statistical comparisons which have no direct relationship, like size of building, for example, which can be placed at the end of the tabulations. All of the comparisons would be gathered together using both sides of a single sheet of paper without a written explanation and will serve as a point of discussion when the material is presented to the library board. Because the information will also be made available to persons who are not library trustees, library jargon should be eliminated. Once again, simplified terminology should be the rule, not the exception.

After determining the strengths and weaknesses of the Anytown Public Library, the librarian decided to compare the following statistics: expenditures, materials budgets, expenditures for video-cassettes, total number of volumes in the libraries, volumes added during the year, magazine subscriptions, use of materials, hours of opening, number of staff members, expenditures for salaries and wages, expenditures for staff fringe benefits, building square footage, and amounts of money received as gifts and memorials to the library during the year. This would give a total of 13 tables in addition to the listing by population.

In working with the statistics from the state library, however, the Anytown librarian discovered that many of the statistics were presented in different ways. Should she make a table for total expenditures or should she tabulate expenditures on a per capita basis? Or should she make two tables? The same was true for expenditures for materials and volumes in the collection. She decided to be open-minded about this and not limit the study to a given number of comparisons.

A table comparing populations should be the first one to appear in the study and, when presented to the board, the librarian needs to explain how the libraries in the group were selected, noting especially when any of them did not meet the original population criterion, with an explanation as to why they were included. Following the population table, Anytown's comparisons would include the following five rankings concerned with library finances: total expenditures, expenditures per capita, materials budget, materials budget per capita, and video expenditures. These comparisons would look like Figure 11-2.

It is important to note not just the relative position of the Anytown Library in each of the comparative tables but also how far they are from the top and bottom figures. Under expenditures per capita, for example, Anytown is fourth best in the ranking, but they are just $1.75 higher than Iron City, the lowest library in the comparison, and nearly $2.00 lower than Pleasantridge at the top. You might wish to compute an average for each ranking (by adding the total for all libraries and dividing by the number of libraries) to enable your board to assess its relative position in the rankings more precisely. The average materials budget per capita is $3.00, for example, placing the Anytown Library just a little above the average for the libraries surveyed. If you decided to compute an average for the libraries' video expenditures, you might wish to consider dropping the two libraries (Iron City and Northland) which did not spend any money for videos because factoring them into the average would lower the figure and make the Anytown Library's expenditures seem better than they actually were.[3] An "average" is a measurement everyone will understand. You should avoid using statistical measurements like "the median," for example, which are poorly understood by many people. You are seeking to present a clear and concise picture of your library by comparing it to others in similar communities. This purpose should guide you when compiling the figures which make up your comparative survey.

FIGURE 11-2   Population Comparison Table

Populations

Northland	15,037
Fairpark	11,987
Green Meadow	11,255
Iron City	10,766
Landview	10,410
ANYTOWN	10,000
Mountaintop	9,381
Hilltown	8,147
Pleasantridge	5,421

Total Expenditures

Mountaintop	$196,750
Green Meadow	139,900
Landview	127,700
ANYTOWN	122,500
Northland	121,000
Fairpark	106,540
Pleasantridge	101,900
Iron City	75,455
Hilltown	49,650

Expenditures per capita

Mountaintop	$20.97
Pleasantridge	18.80
Green Meadow	12.43
Landview	12.27
ANYTOWN	12.25
Fairpark	8.89
Northland	7.87
Iron City	7.01
Hilltown	6.09

Materials budget

Mountaintop	$41,000
Landview	35,000
ANYTOWN	32,000
Green Meadow	31,000
Pleasantridge	28,000
Northland	25,000
Fairpark	24,500
Hilltown	24,500
Iron City	15,000

Materials budget per capita

Pleasantridge	$5.17
Mountaintop	4.37
Landview	3.36
ANYTOWN	3.20
Hilltown	3.01
Green Meadow	2.75
Fairpark	2.04
Northland	1.66
Iron City	1.45

Expenditures for video

Mountaintop	$4,400
Pleasantridge	3,150
Green Meadow	2,300
Landview	1,200
Fairpark	1,000
ANYTOWN	800
Hilltown	500
Northland	0
Iron City	0

The Anytown librarian anticipated that the library's appropriations and materials budget would be comparatively good, but the rankings show instead that on these measures the library is in the middle part of the rankings. Her prediction that the Anytown Library's budget included too little for videos was valid, however, and a good case could be made for increasing this area of the library's budget. Of the libraries spending money for videos, only Hilltown spent less than the Anytown Library, and Anytown was $2,650 lower than the top library in this category.

The next series of rankings, Figure 11-3, relate to collection size and include book volumes in the collection, book volumes per capita, book volumes added during the year, and magazines subscriptions.

The Anytown Library ranks quite well in terms of collection size. In fact it was in third place on all three book volume measures. Size of collection, of course, is a quantity measure and does not necessarily mean quality. But it is a useful comparison to make between libraries serving similar populations. Note that there is not always a direct correlation between volumes in the collection and volumes per capita. While the Anytown Library was third on both measures, Fairpark was the only other library to show this relationship. For some libraries in the study, there was a much wider variation. Pleasantridge, for example, was fifth in total volumes, but first in volumes per capita. The Anytown Library could easily move up in these rankings by increasing its book budget. Anytown is only 4,000 volumes short of being the largest library in the group and added more volumes during the year than the Green Meadow Library, which currently has 2,300 more total volumes than the Anytown Library. The Anytown library board would probably see this fact as an opportunity for advancement. An increase in the materials budget—even a small one—could produce noticeable results the following year (assuming, of course, that the Green Meadow Library does not also have an increase in its materials expenditures).

Two measures of circulation were included in the survey, although the Anytown librarian might also have chosen to compare video circulation since that is one of the areas of appropriations she wishes to improve. Anytown's total circulation was the second highest in the survey but its hold on this position seems rather precarious since Pleasantridge is just 1,085 behind and Green Meadow just 2,345. After seeing the statistics on circulation, the Anytown librarian decided to figure the rate of turnover for each library's collection. The turnover ratio is determined by dividing

FIGURE 11-3   Ranking the Collection

Book volumes in collection		Book volumes per capita	
Mountaintop	51,310	Pleasantridge	7.60
Green Meadow	49,401	Mountaintop	5.47
ANYTOWN	47,112	ANYTOWN	4.71
Northland	46,348	Green Meadow	4.39
Pleasantridge	41,219	Landview	3.42
Fairpark	39,356	Fairpark	3.28
Landview	35,644	Northland	3.08
Iron City	21,775	Hilltown	2.52
Hilltown	20,548	Iron City	2.02

Book volumes added		Magazine subscriptions	
Mountaintop	4,209	Mountaintop	231
Landview	3,302	Green Meadow	200
ANYTOWN	3,007	Pleasantridge	185
Green Meadow	2,932	Northland	171
Fairpark	2,540	ANYTOWN	168
Pleasantridge	2,467	Fairpark	166
Northland	2,121	Landview	156
Hilltown	1,998	Hilltown	79
Iron City	1,491	Iron City	41

the total circulation for each library by the number of volumes in its collection. The resulting table looked like Figure 11-4.

The turnover ratio provides insight into both the quantity and quality of the collection by showing how many times, on average, each item in the collection is being loaned. A low score on this measurement might indicate a need for extensive weeding since the materials are not being borrowed heavily, but the opposite might telegraph the need for a larger collection since the turnover rate is high—meaning the collection is being used extensively. The ratio must be used in conjunction with other measures of library adequacy to know exactly what is being indicated.

Four measures relating to library personnel which make for easy comparisons are hours open per week, staff in full-time equivalents (FTE), salaries and wages, and fringe benefits (Figure 11-5).

There is a relationship, of course, between the number of hours a library is open to the public and the salaries and wages paid to the library staff. But library personnel often work when the library is closed, so the relationship between the two measures is not abso-

---

FIGURE 11-4   Measures of Circulation

Magazines loaned		All materials loaned		Turnover of materials	
Mountaintop	11,844	Mountaintop	121,543	Landview	2.52
ANYTOWN	9,001	ANYTOWN	103,784	Pleasantridge	2.49
Green Meadow	8,891	Pleasantridge	102,699	Hilltown	2.42
Pleasantridge	7,740	Green Meadow	101,439	Mountaintop	2.37
Fairpark	5,129	Northland	98,560	ANYTOWN	2.20
Landview	4,530	Landview	89,666	Iron City	2.20
Iron City	2,319	Fairpark	79,444	Northland	2.13
Hilltown	1,193	Hilltown	50,234	Green Meadow	2.05
Northland	0	Iron City	48,005	Fairpark	2.02

FIGURE 11-5   Table of Hours and Staff

Hours open per week

Fairpark	62
Mountaintop	60
Northland	58
Green Meadow	56
ANYTOWN	52
Landview	52
Pleasantridge	46
Hilltown	44
Iron City	36

Staff in FTE

Mountaintop	5.50
Green Meadow	4.50
Northland	4.25
Landview	3.25
ANYTOWN	3.00
Fairpark	3.00
Pleasantridge	2.85
Hilltown	2.75
Iron City	2.50

Salaries & Wages

Mountaintop	$101,245
Green Meadow	72,990
Landview	65,455
ANYTOWN	62,322
Northland	62,200
Fairpark	60,175
Pleasantridge	55,248
Iron City	45,020
Hilltown	41,000

Fringe benefits

Mountaintop	$15,455
Landview	12,400
Green Meadow	9,500
Northland	9,100
Pleasantridge	8,950
Fairpark	7,850
ANYTOWN	7,702
Iron City	7,692
Hilltown	6,625

lute. Perhaps a more accurate comparison can be made by dividing the total amount spent for salaries and wages by the number of staff members in full-time equivalents. Such a comparison is intriguing in this example because while the Anytown Library is in the middle of the group in terms of total amount spent for wages and salaries, they hold the top place in a ranking of salary per full-time equivalent employee. The Anytown librarian's contention that salaries and wages at the Anytown Library were comparatively low would certainly not stand up if Figure 11-6 were included in the comparisons presented to the library board. The suggestion that fringe benefits were also quite low when compared to other libraries would probably hold up, but it would be circumspect to divide the total spent for fringe benefits by the number of library employees in full-time equivalents.

On this comparative measure the Anytown Library ranks in almost the same position (sixth instead of seventh) as it did in terms of total amount spent for fringe benefits, so the Anytown librarian could draw up a recommendation for an increase in this area of the budget. This data could be used along with fringe benefits determined by a salary survey (which would show exactly what benefits employees of other libraries enjoy which the Anytown staff does not receive) to make recommendations to the library board at budget time.

The last two comparative tables the Anytown librarian produced from the mass of annual statistics available to her were for building square footage, and gifts and memorials received by the Library (Figure 11-8).

The fact that the Anytown Public Library has the second largest building in the comparative survey should act as a stimulus to the library board because it is a measure of potential. The trustees *should* react by desiring to bring the library up to that position on the other measures of library adequacy where Anytown is clearly lagging. There is no guarantee, of course, that the board *will* react this way. Library boards are very unpredictable, to say the least. At the same time, this table congratulates the board for its one shining achievement, a large building. Bear in mind that square footage, like number of volumes, is a measure of quantity not quality. It may be that both Northland and Anytown have older, deteriorating buildings which are no longer attractive to the population they serve, while one of the smaller buildings like Iron City's could be a modern, fully utilized building. The table for gifts and memorials places the Anytown Library once again in the middle area. This ranking should also give impetus to the board by showing what other similar libraries have been able to do in this area, and especially what has been accomplished by the much smaller community of Pleasantridge.

For each library in the comparisons, a profile emerges. The Anytown librarian predicted high scores on appropriations, building size, materials budget, size of collections, and circulation for Anytown. This was correct on building size where the Anytown Library was second only to the much larger town of Northland in terms of building square footage, and also in terms of circulation where Anytown was second to Mountaintop, but the position was a very tenuous one because both Pleasantridge and Green Meadow had only slightly less total circulation. On the other three measures of library adequacy (appropriations, materials budget, and size of collection) the Anytown Library was in the middle group of five libraries making up the "average" position. The Anytown librarian was more accurate in predicting the library's weaknesses. Video expenditures *were* low compared to the other libraries who had video collections (Northland and Iron City did not have them); the number of magazine subscriptions was average; Anytown was fourth best in wages and salaries; staff fringe benefits were also comparatively low; and the number of staff members was just average.

The message coming from these comparisons for the Anytown Library's Board of Trustees is that they are producing a library of only minimal adequacy when compared to other libraries in the state serving similar populations. On some measures they are doing a better job than the much larger town of Northland, but on others they are being out-distanced by the much smaller town of Pleasantridge. Few boards of trustees are complacent enough to accept mediocrity for their libraries. Most, upon seeing comparisons like these, will seek to make improvements so that next year their library will move up terms of library adequacy.

DRAWING CONCLUSIONS

It is important to remember that each library's position in the rankings can be used with one's library board to the advantage of the library. It doesn't matter where your library falls in the comparisons. Ideally, you will start at the bottom of the heap and work your way upward as you improve your library's adequacy on the various measures, but every library is not going to be in that position. The Mountaintop librarian, for example, would find her

FIGURE 11-6   Salary per FTE

Annual cost per full-time library employee

ANYTOWN	$20,774
Landview	20,140
Fairpark	20,058
Pleasantridge	19,385
Mountaintop	18,408
Iron City	18,008
Green Meadow	16,220
Hilltown	14,909
Northland	14,635

FIGURE 11-7   Benefits per FTE

Fringe benefits per FTE library employee

Landview	$3,815
Pleasantridge	3,140
Iron City	3,077
Mountaintop	2,810
Fairpark	2,617
ANYTOWN	2,567
Hilltown	2,409
Northland	2,141
Green Meadow	2,111

FIGURE 11-8   Building Size, Gifts and Memorials

Building square feet		Gifts & memorials	
Northland	12,000	Pleasantridge	$6,400
ANYTOWN	10,000	Green Meadow	4,351
Mountaintop	9,350	Fairpark	3,100
Green Meadow	9,000	Landview	2,545
Fairpark	8,500	ANYTOWN	1,250
Pleasantridge	7,550	Mountaintop	956
Landview	6,200	Northland	827
Iron City	5,000	Hilltown	824
Hilltown	4,800	Iron City	423

library to be at or near the top on practically every measure and must convince the trustees to continue the efforts which have made their library a superior one. Her strategy with the board would be different from that of the Iron City librarian whose library is at the bottom in nearly every measure and needs to push for improvement in so many different areas. Both would be different from the strategy appropriate for the Anytown librarian whose library is in the middle on most measures, but has room to improve in just about every way.

My own experience has been one of starting at the bottom and rapidly moving to the top. The strategy used with my board changed as improvements were made. At first, it was very obvious that our library needed drastic help and we began with appropriations. By using comparisons with 12 other Iowa public libraries I was able to persuade the board to increase the book budget by 500 percent in my second year as librarian. Our book budget went from eleventh to second best that year, and on a per capita basis we were tops. Other improvements were evident in that year's rankings as well. We improved in total expenditures, hours of opening, number of employees, magazine subscriptions, salaries and wages, book volumes, and volumes added during the year. The changes we made as a result of comparing our library with others in similar sized communities produced lasting effects and contributed to 23 straight years of circulation gains. As the library's adequacy on all measures increased, the board became more and more enthusiastic about the library and it actually became easier for me to push for further progress in all areas of the library's operation. When we reached the top there was no thought of relaxing to catch our breath. The board was caught up in the process and continued to look for ways to improve the library.

SPREADING THE WORD

All of the comparative tables are put together on one sheet of paper for presentation to the library board, the sources of public revenue, and the media. You should try to limit the data to two sides of a letter size paper. Your ability to do so, naturally, will be determined by the number of libraries you compare your library to as well as the number of different measures used. Once again, simplicity should be your guideline. You don't want to confuse the very people you wish to persuade to make needed library improvements possible. If you are unable to get all of your tables on an 8 1/2 by 11 inch paper and you feel that all of your chosen measures are important, you may wish to use legal size paper. The final comparison study made by the Anytown librarian looked like Figure 11-9.

SPREADING THE WORD TO THE LIBRARY BOARD
The annual comparison of library statistics will be greeted with enthusiasm if your library board sees it as an opportunity to plan for future library improvements. The item is placed on the agenda of a regular board meeting (usually the same one each year due to the regularity of the data's availability). Keep in mind that your purpose is to show how your library compares with others in communities of your size. Resist the temptation to belittle other libraries in the study which may be substandard on many of the measures.

It is better not to muddy the issue with a written commentary about the rankings. The comparisons, if presented without comment (other than during the first year's presentation when selection criteria are given), will stimulate trustee discussion. This does not mean that the librarian cannot comment on the measures and the library's position, just that it be kept verbal and to a minimum. Trustees will need to be guided through the tables with relationships between rankings and/or each one's significance commented upon. My first presentation to my board of trustees was met with dead silence. I believe they were in a state of shock because our library fared so poorly on nearly all of the measures and the trustees had not realized how bad their library really was. But it proved to be a turning point for the library because, even though there was not much dicussion when the statistics were presented, trustees often referred back to them when coming to terms with needed library improvements at subsequent meetings.

As the years pass and the library moves up in the rankings, your library trustees can actually see that their actions on the library's behalf are bringing results. This is the reason you will want to present the comparisons year after year. One of the problems with public libraries is that it is difficult to measure library improvements—to translate the effort the trustees expend into measurable factors. Circulation figures alone do not tell the story of library improvements. In fact, circulation may decline because of factors beyond the control of the library staff or board. This is especially true in the smaller community where a severe winter or a school curriculum change might easily lower a public library's circulation of materials. The rankings of libraries serving similar populations, on the other hand, are a very visible means of illustrating library improvements.

SPREADING THE WORD TO THE REVENUE SOURCES

You can use the comparative statistics for your library as an effective means of gaining increased revenue from your various sources of funding. Just as library trustees hate to see their library looking average or worse, the same perception is generally true for those who control the library's financial support. People don't want to be average in anything and this applies to members of the city and county government boards just as it does to library trustees. Remember that you are in control of the statistical measures you present. You may wish to add a table comparing city appropriations for the library if you feel the city (or any other governmental jurisdiction from which you receive operating funds) is comparatively low. In the same way, you may wish to exclude data which would be detrimental to your cause.

At the Carroll Library, for example, my board and I worked

hard to get county appropriations high enough to match use made of the library by county residents. When we finally reached that level, however, a table ranking our comparison libraries showed our library to be much higher on this measure than any of the other libraries simply because those libraries in our comparative pool had not been successful in getting increased appropriations from this source. Since we did not wish to appear to have more county money than other libraries and risk a possible cut in funding, we chose not to include this table when the comparisons were distributed to the county board.

It is a good idea to present the information at budget time when the statistics are fresh in the memory and may be used to request increased funding for the library. The material is best presented, along with the budget request, by the president of the library board, the chair of its financial committee, or both (with the library director close at hand for clarification, if needed). It doesn't matter where your library falls in the rankings—support for your budget request can be made no matter how you rate in comparison to other libraries. It may be easier to get an increase if your library is below average, but a skillful trustee can use high rankings as a way of saying thank you for past support and weave in a plea for increased funds to help maintain the library's high level. Be sure that you make a copy of the rankings for each member of the governmental agency—this is information you definitely want to spread around!

SPREADING THE WORD TO THE PUBLIC

The comparative rankings are tailor-made for the media. You may wish to write an article about the comparisons for the media sources in your community or you may seek an interview with a reporter. The information about your library and how it compares to its peers will be of great interest in the community both to library users and nonusers alike. As your library raises its level of adequacy and the media reports on this achievement, more nonusers will seek out the library, which will in turn lead to more improvements and corresponding gains for the library in terms of more usership. Community pride is a powerful force and it can be used to the library's advantage by making known to the public exactly how good the library is and how it has improved over the previous year. Comparative statistics will make this possible. It is a very effective and often neglected way of initiating improvements in all areas of a public library's program.

FIGURE 11-9   Compiling all the Tables

COMPARISON OF LIBRARY STATISTICS
FOR NINE PUBLIC LIBRARIES
FOR FISCAL YEAR 1991
As Reported by the State Library

Population		Total expenditures		Expenditures per capita	
Northland	15,037	Mountaintop	$196,750	Mountaintop	$20.97
Fairpark	11,987	Green Meadow	139,900	Pleasantridge	18.80
Green Meadow	11,255	Landview	127,700	Green Meadow	12.43
Iron City	10,766	ANYTOWN	122,500	Landview	12.27
Landview	10,410	Northland	121,000	ANYTOWN	12.25
ANYTOWN	10,000	Fairpark	106,540	Fairpark	8.89
Mountaintop	9,381	Pleasantridge	101,900	Northland	7.87
Hilltown	8,147	Iron City	75,455	Iron City	7.01
Pleasantridge	5,421	Hilltown	49,650	Hilltown	6.09

Materials budget		Materials budget per capita		Expenditures for video	
Mountaintop	$41,000	Pleasantridge	$5.17	Mountaintop	$4,400
Landview	35,000	Mountaintop	4.37	Pleasantridge	3,150
ANYTOWN	32,000	Landview	3.36	Green Meadow	2,300
Green Meadow	31,000	ANYTOWN	3.20	Landview	1,200
Pleasantridge	28,000	Hilltown	3.01	Fairpark	1,000
Northland	25,000	Green Meadow	2.75	ANYTOWN	800
Fairpark	24,500	Fairpark	2.04	Hilltown	500
Hilltown	24,500	Northland	1.66	Northland	0
Iron City	15,000	Iron City	1.45	Iron City	0

Continued

FIGURE 11-9 *Continued*

Book volumes in collection

Mountaintop	51,310
Green Meadow	49,401
ANYTOWN	47,112
Northland	46,348
Pleasantridge	41,219
Fairpark	39,356
Landview	35,644
Iron City	21,775
Hilltown	20,548

Book volumes per capita

Pleasantridge	7.60
Mountaintop	5.47
ANYTOWN	4.71
Green Meadow	4.39
Landview	3.42
Fairpark	3.28
Northland	3.08
Hilltown	2.52
Iron City	2.02

Book volumes added during year

Mountaintop	4,209
Landview	3,302
ANYTOWN	3,007
Green Meadow	2,932
Fairpark	2,540
Pleasantridge	2,467
Northland	2,121
Hilltown	1,998
Iron City	1,491

Magazine subsriptions

Mountaintop	231
Green Meadow	200
Pleasantridge	185
Northland	171
ANYTOWN	168
Fairpark	166
Landview	156
Hilltown	79
Iron City	41

Magazines loaned

Mountaintop	11,844
ANYTOWN	9,001
Green Meadow	8,891
Pleasantridge	7,740
Fairpark	5,129
Landview	4,530
Iron City	2,319
Hilltown	1,193
Northland	0

All materials loaned

Mountaintop	121,543
ANYTOWN	103,784
Pleasantridge	102,699
Green Meadow	101,439
Northland	98,560
Landview	89,666
Fairpark	79,444
Hilltown	50,234
Iron City	48,005

Continued

FIGURE 11-9 *Continued*

Turnover of materials	
Landview	2.52
Pleasantridge	2.49
Hilltown	2.42
Mounaintop	2.37
ANYTOWN	2.20
Iron City	2.20
Northland	2.13
Green Meadow	2.05
Fairpark	2.02

Hours open per week	
Fairpark	62
Mountaintop	60
Northland	58
Green Meadow	56
ANYTOWN	52
Landview	52
Pleasantridge	46
Hilltown	44
Iron City	36

Staff in FTE	
Mountaintop	5.50
Green Meadow	4.50
Northland	4.25
Landview	3.25
ANYTOWN	3.00
Fairpark	3.00
Pleasantridge	2.85
Hilltown	2.75
Iron City	2.50

Salaries & wages	
Mountaintop	$101,245
Green Meadow	72,990
Landview	64,455
ANYTOWN	62,322
Northland	62,200
Fairpark	60,175
Pleasantridge	55,248
Iron City	45,020
Hilltown	41,000

Salary & wage cost per full-time employee	
ANYTOWN	$20,744
Landview	20,140
Fairpark	20,058
Pleasantridge	19,385
Mountaintop	18,408
Iron City	18,008
Green Meadow	16,220
Hilltown	14,909
Northland	14,635

Fringe benefits	
Mountaintop	$15,455
Landview	12,400
Green Meadow	9,500
Northland	9,100
Pleasantridge	8,950
Fairpark	7,850
ANYTOWN	7,702
Iron City	7,692
Hilltown	6,625

Continued

FIGURE 11-9 *Continued*

Fringe benefits per full-time employee		Building size in square feet		Gifts & memorials received	
Landview	$3,815	Northland	12,000	Pleasantridge	$6,400
Pleasantridge	3,140	ANYTOWN	10,000	Green Meadow	4,351
Iron City	3,077	Mountaintop	9,350	Fairpark	3,100
Mountaintop	2,810	Green Meadow	9,000	Landview	2,545
Fairpark	2,617	Fairpark	8,500	ANYTOWN	1,250
ANYTOWN	2,567	Pleasantridge	7,550	Mountaintop	956
Hilltown	2,409	Landview	6,200	Northland	827
Northland	2,141	Iron City	5,000	Hilltown	824
Green Meadow	2,111	Hilltown	4,800	Iron City	423

SUMMARY

Library boards have very few tools to measure the level of adequacy achieved by the libraries they control. Statistical comparison with other libraries serving similar populations is a good way to illustrate comparative excellence or mediocrity. By using data readily available to them, library directors and trustees may make library comparisons and use this information to improve all aspects of the library in their community. The information from a comparative study of this nature can also be used effectively to publicize the library, its achievements, and its needs.

ENDNOTES

1. Irvin H. Sherman, "What Makes a Library Well Run?" *Canadian Library Journal,* October 1984: 232.

2. "In April 1988, Congress directed that there be an annual collection of public library statistics by the National Center for Education Statistics (NCES)." U.S. National Commission on Libraries and Information Science, *Wanted— Facts About Public Libraries: An Action Plan for a New Federal/State Cooperative System.* National Center for Education Statistics. U.S. Government Printing Office, 1989: 3.

3. Shirley George, state librarian, *Iowa Public Library Statistics 1988-1989.* Des Moines, IA: The State Library of Iowa, 1989.

4. The average using all eight libraries would be $1,519 while the average using only those six libraries who actually spent money on videos during the year would be $2,025.

12 THE FUTURE OF LIBRARY BOARDS

Library boards have been in existence for over 2,000 years. Their evolution has been from absolute power over the destiny of the library it controls to a role of only partial control. As libraries became more complex, boards increasingly needed to delegate their powers to an administrator or library manager. In modern libraries, some boards have lost their powers and become advisory boards while others have been eliminated completely with control given to municipal managers. Board power would appear to be declining. One might well ask if the library board has a future.

THE IDEAL BOARD

In the ideal library board/library director relationship there exists a spirit of cooperation, mutual trust, and hard work directed toward a common goal: library improvement. As a library director from Idaho put it: "I acknowledge the library board as the holders of ultimate responsibility and therefore authority and I demand that they acknowledge me as the manager and expert on library issues. We need each other and should work with each other to achieve the goals we have set for the library." The library board stays within its boundaries as policy maker and the library director applies these policies to the library and its operation. The board has its duties and the director has his or her duties; there is no blurring of roles, no crossover into the other's area of operation. The library director is given broad discretionery powers which are carefully exercised. The board aggressively seeks funding for the library and the library director prudently spends this money to raise the library to a state of excellence. The library board is supportive of its director and the director, in turn, applauds the efforts of the board. The board recognizes the effectiveness of its director and rewards it with a salary which is commensurate with performance. In short, there is a sort of "mutual admiration society" which leads to a superior library where the board and director work together in a congenial way.

This is the board/director relationship in its ideal state. I know of no public library where this situation is the norm at all times. Many directors and boards work harmoniously, but I know from talking to other library directors that the library board/library director relationship is not always a smooth one.

It would be interesting to know how many library directors feel that they have a reasonable, if not ideal, working relationship with their library boards. We tend to hear about those boards and directors who are not getting along very well, but we don't hear about the majority who work in harmony. We don't know how many libraries are being operated by library boards and library directors who get along well with one another and cooperatively produce good libraries. It is not the good news which gets reported.

Library trustees are in a difficult position. They are charged with the control of the library, yet they must delegate much of their authority to a paid library director. Trustees are considered to be effective if they manage and control their libraries, yet in doing so they may cross over into areas perceived by library directors as their jurisdictions.[1] Boards deal with policy and decision-making but do not always understand where their job ends and the director's job begins. They have legal responsibilities and can be sued if they don't perform these responsibilities properly.[2] Being a library trustee is not an easy job and library directors need to support them just as we seek their support.

TWO VIEWS OF THE RELATIONSHIP

Who is to blame for the fact that some library directors and library boards are at odds with each other and are not working in the best interests of the libraries they serve? On the one side is the view that library directors seek to run their libraries as if their boards did not exist. "The library director does not want to take the chance that by allowing the trustees to get active he or she might lose partial control of the library operation to an 'outsider.'"[3] The other view is that library boards want to take over the roles of library directors and regress to the style of management of the ancient libraries where the librarian was just a custodian of books. "And then there are Those Other Boards. One hears about them from colleagues. They, too, are trying to do their duty as they see it, but they combine bossiness, ignorance, and caprice in equal parts. They seek to run the library themselves using you as a glorified clerk."[4]

The blame for an unproductive relationship between board and director is one which must be shared by both groups. Library directors need to believe that library boards serve a useful and necessary function in the decision-making process which will lead to a better library. Library boards need to believe that their role is one of governing the way the library operates, not directing that operation. Roles need to be defined in libraries where the director and board are in conflict. Trustees and directors need to communicate if they are to have a productive relationship.

Library boards can be educated to understand and perform the roles given them by the state and local laws which legalize their powers. But library directors must yield to those powers and allow boards to function effectively. Mutual understanding and cooperation are needed if the library is to serve its public in the best possible way.

WHEN THINGS GO WRONG

There will be times in every library director's tenure when his or her relationship with the board of trustees goes awry. To deal effectively with the problem, its existence must first be recognized. At that point, steps must be taken to resolve the conflict before resolution becomes impossible. Communication is the essential ingredient needed to bring about a compromise which leads to a righting of the board/director relationship. There may be times when the conflict is not resolvable, and the library director must recognize these situations as well. Unfortunately there are library boards who cannot get along with any director. We all know of these public libraries because their directors never stay long enough to improve the library. When I was a student in library science at the University of Minnesota I was made acutely aware of a public library in the nearby state of Wisconsin where the director changed every year. It was an instance of a library board which was too powerful. Many of the trustees were officers of national corporations. They attempted to run their city's public library as they ran their companies and no library director could work with them. It was an unworkable situation.

Impasses between boards and directors do happen in public libraries. My survey found at least two situations of this nature. In one the board had been unable to prevent a drastic cut in the library's budget and in the other, a library director in the New England area stated: "I am seriously considering leaving because the board is extremely authoritative and I cannot work well with supervisors like that. Three are very high-pressure, take-charge, domineering types. One sits firmly on the fence. Two usually support me and number seven is brand new—no way to know where she'll head." We must accept the fact that some board/ director situations cannot be resolved and the librarian has little choice but to seek another position. At times like these it can be very beneficial to talk to other library directors. When one is having "board problems" of any type, a meeting with one's peers is good for it often alters your perspective. I always come away from my biannual meetings with other library directors at ILOMS (Iowa Libraries of Medium Size) with a changed outlook and renewed hope from listening to others tell of their problems!

SUPPORTIVE BOARDS

Most library directors recognize that their library boards are here to stay. "Boards, whether governing or advisory, are a fact of life. You can't have your board abolished, so you must work with it. If properly handled, it can be helpful. Members can lobby the government that pays your bills, they can talk up the library in their social and business circles, they can convey public sentiment to you, and they can support you in bad times, the fiscal and censorship incidents."[5] Every director, being honest about it, can point to a time of thankfulness for the support of the library board. Members can be a reliable buffer between the director and an antagonistic adversary from the community. They will often influence, in ways that you cannot, legislators and government officials who control your library's money supply. They may serve as a friendly advisor when things are going badly and give you a lift when you need it the most.

The library board can be extremely valuable when things go wrong "for sometimes the librarian simply does not have enough perceived authority to deal with the problem."[6] But will the library board be there when you need it? Not too many years ago it would have been unthinkable that library boards could indeed be abolished, yet an attempt to do so occurred in Iowa. The measure was defeated by a unified coalition of librarians, trustees, and library users, but the fact that the legislation was proposed at all is an ominous development for the future of public libraries in America. This was not an isolated incident. In South Carolina a county council attempted to take over a library board's powers by passing a local ordinance and the same the same thing happened in

Bloomfield, Iowa.[7,8] Both attempts were overturned by state attorney generals. One would hope that this is not something which foreshadows the future of library boards.

SOME FINAL THOUGHTS

Library boards working with library directors for improvements in library collections, services, and programs is a practical concept which works. To every rule, however, there will always be exceptions. There will be libraries where the director and board do not work cooperatively with each other. There will be libraries where the board takes over responsibilities and duties of the library director, and there will be libraries where the director takes over the decision and policy making functions of the board. But these instances are exceptions—they are not common everyday occurences.

"The benefits of working with a library committee (board) far outweigh the liabilities."[9] A Virginia library director stated: "The working relationship with a board is an essential part of good library administration." The key is to work with your library board and to educate them in every phase of the library operation so that they can make positive decisions and, together, you and your board can make your library the best possible library for the community you serve.

ENDNOTES

1. Daniel W. Casey, "Quality and Quantity of Public Library Service Depend on Trustees." *Public Libraries* 24, no. 1, Spring 1985: 3.

2. "Trustee Legal Liability Defined by ALA Counsel" *Library Journal* 104, no. 22, December 15, 1979: 2608.

3. Will Manley, "Facing the Public: 'Our Libraries are Fundamentally in the Hands of Our Trustees.'" *Wilson Library Bulletin,* 61, no. 9, May 1987: 30.

4. William A. Katz, ed. *The How-To-Do-It Manual for Small Libraries.* New York: Neal-Schuman Publishers Inc., 1987. p. 6.

5. Katz, pp. 5-6.

6. Guy St. Clair, "The Library Committee: Powerful Advocate? . . .Or More Trouble Than It's Worth?" *The One-Person Library: a Newsletter for Librarians & Management* 5, no. 11, March 1989: 1.

7. "Trustee Victory in S.C. Bars County Council Rule," *Library Journal* 108, no. 18, October 15, 1983: 1905.

8. Lynn M. Walding, Assistant Attorney General."Opinion of the Attorney General Regarding a Proposed Ordinance of the Bloomfield, Iowa, City Council." pp. 1-2.

9. Jane H. Katayama, "The Library Committee How Important Is It?" *Special Libraries,* 24, no. 1, January 1983: 45.

BIBLIOGRAPHY

BOOKS

Altman, Ellen, ed. *Local Public Library Administration,* 2nd ed. Chicago: American Library Association, 1980.

Alvarez, Robert S. *Library Boss; Thoughts on Library Personnel.* South San Francisco, CA: Administrator's Digest Press, 1987.

Auger, B.Y. *How to Run More Effective Business Meetings.* New York: Grosset & Dunlap, 1964.

Brilhart, John K. *Effective Group Discussion.* 5th ed. Dubuque, IA: William C. Brown, 1986.

Drucker, Peter F. *The Effective Executive.* New York: Harper and Row, 1967.

————. *Managing the Nonprofit Organization.* New York: HarperCollins Publishers, 1990.

Duca, Diane J. *Nonprofit Boards: A Practical Guide to Roles, Responsibilities, and Performance.* Phoenix, AZ: The Oryx Press, 1986.

Edsall, Marian B. *Library Promotion Handbook.* Phoenix, AZ: The Oryx Press, 1980.

Ihrig, Alice B. *Decision-Making for Public Libraries.* Hamden, CT: The Shoestring Press, 1989.

Iowa Public Library Statistics 1988-1989. Des Moines, IA: The State Library of Iowa, 1989.

Joeckel, Carleton B. *The Government of the American Public Library.* Chicago: University of Chicago Press, 1948.

Katz, William A., ed. *The How-To-Do-It Manual for Small Libraries.* New York: Neal-Schuman Publishers, Inc., 1987.

Kohn, Rita and Tepper, Krysta. *You Can Do It.* Metuchen, NJ: Scarecrow Press, 1981.

Leigh, Robert D. *The Public Library in the United States.* New York: Columbia University Press, 1950.

Pungitore, Verna L. *Public Librarianship; An Issues-oriented Approach.* Westport, CT: Greenwood Press, Inc., 1989.

Ross, Catherine S. and Dewdney, Patricia. *Communicating Professionally.* New York: Neal-Schuman Publishers, Inc., 1989.

Rummel, Kathleen K. and Perica, Esther, eds. *Persuasive Public Relations for Libraries*. Chicago: American Library Association, 1983.

Sager, Donald J. *Managing the Public Library*. White Plains, NY: Knowledge Industry Publications Inc., 1984.

St. Clair, Guy and Williamson, Joan. *Managing the One-Person Library*. London: Butterworth & Co. (Publishers) Ltd., 1986.

Shera, Jesse H. *Foundations of the Public Library*. Chicago: University of Chicago Press, 1948.

Sherman, Steve. *ABC's of Library Promotion*, 2nd ed. Metuchen, NJ: Scarecrow Press, Inc., 1980.

State Standards Committee. *In Service to Iowa: Public Measures of Quality*. 2nd ed. Des Moines: State Library of Iowa, 1989.

Thompson, James W. *Ancient Libraries*. Berkeley, CA: University of California Press, 1940.

Thomsett, Michael C. *The Little Black Book of Business Meetings*. New York: American Management Association, 1989.

Young, Virginia G. *The Library Trustee,* 4th ed. Chicago: American Library Association, 1988.

————. *The Trustee of a Small Public Library*. Chicago: American Library Association, 1978.

ARTICLES

Amundson, William, with Mitchell, Milton. "The Policy Making Role of the System Trustee," *Wisconsin Library Bulletin,* Spring 1984.

Arney, Mary E. "Library Boards—Who They Are and How They Get There," *Show-Me Libraries,* Spring 1988.

Butler, Ellis O. "Confessions of a Fusty Trustee," *The Tennessee Librarian* 38, no. 1, Winter 1986.

Casey, Daniel W. "Quality and Quantity of Public Library Service Depend on Trustees," *Public Libraries* 24, no. 1, Spring 1985.

Franklin, Robert D. "The Administrator and the Board," *Library Trends* 11, no. 1, July 1962.

Galant, Eleanore. "The Public Library Trustee and Changing Community Needs," *The Bookmark*, Summer 1987.

Hobbs, Charles. "Improving Meetings," *Library Administrator's Digest* XXIII, no. 9, November 1988.

Katayama, Jane H. "The Library Committee: How Important Is It?" *Special Libraries* 24, no. 1, January 1983.

Klee, Ed. "The Public Library Board is Looking for a Few Good Trustees," *Kentucky Libraries*, Winter 1989.

Kreamer, Jean T. "The Library Trustee as a Library Activist," in *Public Libraries,* Volume 29, Number 4, July/August 1990.

Lang, Shirley. "The Role and Responsibility of the Public Library Trustee," in *The Bookmark*, Summer 1987.

Lucas, John A. and Madden, Michael. "A Trustee's Guide to Library Budget Building," *The Bottom Line* 3, no. 1.

Lynch, Timothy P. "A Preliminary Survey of Library Board Trustees From Four Libraries in Pennsylvania," *Rural Libraries* VII, no. 2, 1987.

Manley, Will. "Facing the Public: 'Our Public Libraries are Fundamentally in the Hands of Our Trustees," *Wilson Library Bulletin,* 61, no. 9, May 1987.

Roodselaar, Christine van and Prior, Michael. "The Library Trustee: An Alberta Perspective," *Canadian Library Journal*, August 1988.

St. Clair, Guy. "The Library Committee: Powerful Advocate?. . .Or More Trouble Than It's Worth?" *The One-Person Library: A Newsletter For Librarians & Management 5*, no. 11, March 1989.

Schochet, Lois K. "Historical Background," *Library Trends* 11, no. 1, July, 1962.

Sherman, Irvin H. "What Makes a Library Well-Run?" *Canadian Library Journal,* October 1984.

Swan, James. "Inside the System: A Primer For Trustees," *Wilson Library Bulletin* 60, no. 6, February 1986.

"Trustee Legal Liability Defined by ALA Counsel," *Library Journal* 104, no. 22, December 15, 1979.

"Trustee Victory in S.C. Bars County Council Rule," *Library Journal* 108, no. 18, October 15, 1983.

Walding, Lynn M., Assistant Attorney General. "Opinion of the Attorney General Regarding a Proposed Ordinance of the Bloomfield, Iowa, City Council."

"Wanted—Facts About Public Libraries: An Action Plan for a New Federal-State Cooperative System," Washington, D.C., U.S. National Commission on Libraries and Information Science. National Center for Education Statistics. U.S. Government Printing Office, 1989.

Williams, Lorraine M. "Fostering Human Values on a Library Board," *Canadian Library Journal,* August 1986.

Williams, Margaret Ann Bercher and Schlessinger, Bernard S. "The Texas Public Library Trustee," *Public Library Quarterly,* Winter, 1984.

INDEX

Gordon S. Wade is Library Director of the
Carroll Public Library, Carroll, Iowa.

Book design: Gloria Brown
Cover design: Apicella Design
Typography: Roberts/Churcher